"THINK" AND "DO"

IN BUSINESS AND MANAGEMENT

D. RADHAKRISHNAN NAIR

INDIA • SINGAPORE • MALAYSIA

Notion Press

Old No. 38, New No. 6
McNichols Road, Chetpet
Chennai - 600 031

First Published by Notion Press 2019
Copyright © D. Radhakrishnan Nair 2019
All Rights Reserved.

ISBN 978-1-64587-791-2

This book has been published with all efforts taken to make the material error-free after the consent of the author. However, the author and the publisher do not assume and hereby disclaim any liability to any party for any loss, damage, or disruption caused by errors or omissions, whether such errors or omissions result from negligence, accident, or any other cause.

While every effort has been made to avoid any mistake or omission, this publication is being sold on the condition and understanding that neither the author nor the publishers or printers would be liable in any manner to any person by reason of any mistake or omission in this publication or for any action taken or omitted to be taken or advice rendered or accepted on the basis of this work. For any defect in printing or binding the publishers will be liable only to replace the defective copy by another copy of this work then available.

DEDICATION

This book is dedicated to the Patron and Chairman of SCMS Group of Educational Institutions, Dr. G.P.C. Nayar. He has been heading an empire of educational institutions on the SCMS model, training the youth to hone their skills to become nation builders and leaders as executives, technocrats, architects, scientists, and finance managers.

No management guru he emulated. He evolved himself as an impeccable management guru if establishing and sustaining a few management and technological institutions in India can be deemed to be the function of a management guru.

The management journal which this book sprouted from, has been one of the best in India with its indexing and listing level ranging from EBSCO, PROQUEST, J-GATE, ICI, INDEX COPERNICUS, ULRICH'S, CABELL'S DIRECTORY, and now to SCOPUS databases. The SCMS Group has been spending THREE CRORES of rupees for the last fifteen years to establish and sustain this journal and by doing so to eclipse all thirteen universities and national institutes in the state of Kerala in the publication of journals. Among indexed journals in India, SCMS can stake claims as the best.

It's only entrepreneurship and educational vision and wisdom in running international educational institutions in diverse disciplines that culminated in his success.

I have been editing the journal for the last fifteen years. I have compiled all my editorials published to fill in the lacuna of pedagogy components in business and management curriculum in a small way. I dedicate this book *"Think" and "Do" in Business and Management*, to the **great** man Dr. G.P.C. Nayar.

D. Radhakrishnan Nair

CONTENTS

Prologomena .... *ix*
Curtain Raiser .... *xiii*
Overview .... *xv*
Foreword .... *xxi*

1. Nature is the Best Teacher in Management 1
2. Conserve the Lungs of Our Earth! 3
3. Ecology and Culture 5
4. Nature and Human Nature 8
5. Manage the Manna We Get from the Mother Earth ... 11
6. Business and Climate Change 13
7. Culture and Business 15
8. Business Culture 17
9. Culture and Adaptation:
   Imperatives, Electives, and Exclusives 19
10. Cricket/Business: Understanding Culture 22
11. B Techno Culture and Risk 25
12. Sense of Touch and Business 27
13. The Ear and Business 30
14. Smell and Management 33
15. Taste and Management 36

16. Colour and Management..................39
17. Dream-Streaming.........................41
18. Dream-Storming..........................43
19. Working with Our Dreams..................46
20. The "Cave Image" and Learning.............48
21. To Think Critically is to Reason Clearly..........50
22. Management: Ontology and Pedagogy...........52
23. Teaching and Learning.....................54
24. God Manages Cosmos......................56
25. B-School Learning and Teaching...............58
26. Homo Symbolificus.........................60
27. Business and Management: Subject and Predicate...63
28. On the Move: Exhaustion to Replenishment......66
29. Business and Ontology......................68
30. Individual and Society.....................71
31. Strategy as Language Game.................73
32. Rhetoric of Space and Business...............75
33. Welch and Smith and Their Rhetoric............77
34. Psychic Patterns in Business Space 80
35. Journal Potential in Education and Research......82
36. Entrepreneurship and Education 84
37. Holacracy in Academia.....................86
38. Icon, Index, Symbol.......................88
39. Computer Literate and Information Literate.......91
40. Setting Direction, Creating Alignment, and
    Gaining Commitment.......................94
41. New Dawn for Development 97
42. Let the Buyer Beware! 99
43. Super Trends in Business....................101

44. We Bristle When We Are Bridled 104
45. Creativity 106
46. Empower Nurses for Health Care Management... 108
47. Invoke Solar Energy: Save the Universe!......... 111
48. River of Time 113
49. Management, Manager, and Manage............115
50. A Good Manager:
    A Good and Well Educated Person 117
51. B School and Cultural Studies 119
52. Harmony in Triune: Art, Science, and Craft....... 121
53. Lady Justice Under Cyber Threat.............. 123
54. "Mundane" and "Inspiring" 125
55. Myth and Management 127

PROLOGOMENA

Newly minted winter 'b' tips

1.1 These jottings...

These jottings on business and management, scribbled over a decade and a half, during my short tenure in the winter of my career as a faculty in a business school in Cochin, do not tell a unified tale, but they tell of an intellectual trajectory. In the business school, I found myself deeply uncertain about the direction I wanted my work to take on.

1.2 Odourless odour of business...

When I stepped in, I was only mildly interested in the formalist agenda that dominated the post-graduate instruction in business and management imparted to graduates chosen from all over India. Then I felt, even in my sweat, the sweet smell of the "red, red rose that's newly sprung in June." Slowly I underwent a change; the sweat gave way to the odourless order of the odd business ambience.

1.3 Grooming for skilled profession

The dawn of the twenty first century saw a change in the approach of job giver and the job seeker. As business grew by leaps and bounds, the business people found no time in training unskilled youth in management skills. Therefore there was a growing demand for business schools. This resulted in mushrooming of institutions. The managements of such institutions never waited for the comprehension of philosophy and thought behind the academic and research requirements of such business schools.

1.4 Business in business school

What is the business taught and trained in a b-school? Business is not a subject of study for the school. How to manage business is their concern. Already established business corporate wants professionals to sustain their business. Therefore the focus of a business school was reduced to enlighten the raw graduates of various disciplines in managing techniques. Creativity was their limited concern. Marketing of the existing products of the corporate was the sole concern.

1.5 Nothing as certain

"There is nothing as certain as our continual uncertainty," says Philip Sidney and so certain are the cases with regard to the concept of business education all over the world. I wanted to know where would be the beginning of business education. The product, in business, shall evolve out of raw materials. It shall inevitably be a culmination of some change. Where does the process of change commence from? In the beginning, there was only an inevitable chaos. What is the texture of the chaos? What is it made on?

1.6 Ever growing paradox...

The chaos to me is nature: the nature of the ever-growing paradox: the human brain. The human brain, the puzzle, is to solve never-ending trajectory of puzzles. Human brain undertakes to solve the puzzles of nature. It taps, explores, and cultures nature's gifts into products for the wellbeing of the people all over the world. Tapping and culturing are done by human beings for others for which human brain shall be used. The former part is called labour and the latter is management. Tapping and culturing are accompaniments of the human race. Business is changing nature's gifts to useful products for the human race. Business is always progressive. Better tapping and better culturing will produce better product for the race. The role of management comes in the process when man uses brain for business.

1.7 Eye opener

Development of our world hinges on development of world economy, which in turn hangs on development of business. Business and its growth rely on 'good' and 'great' business run by talents in business. Greater growth of business requires greater number of talented people. It's here that b-schools prove their mettle. B-schools choose students with potential talents. They groom them properly. As more talents are essential, more b-schools have been established. B-school offers both teaching and training.

1.8 Business – a cultural imperative

Culture plays a central role in the world. It is not mere wishful thinking. Why does culture play a central role? It is the result of an assessment of the present situation. It is a genuine prediction on the prospects for the future. It transforms the relationship between human beings and the natural environment. It reduces the amount of tension, violence, terrorism, and conflict in this world. It improves relations between diverse peoples, countries, cultures, and religions and civilizations of the world. It decreases income and social inequalities throughout the world. Only culture can reduce man's demands on the world's scarce resources of life. Only it can create ways of life and lifestyles in keeping with the new global reality. Only culture can achieve much more peace, harmony, stability, and unity in the world. It is in this context we are constrained to believe that business is inevitable in the world. Transformation of the relations between human beings and the natural environment is the major cultural imperative.

CURTAIN RAISER

Pedagogy is teaching. It can be the art, or science, or craft of a teacher. At the outset, man starts learning from nature. Nature is then the teacher. The distinguished teacher nature wants her student man to observe her to learn from. It requires man's systematic observation of nature. The mind of man after observing nature starts using the skill of observing to learn more through observation. This helps man in closely understanding nature. This at once helps man in whetting the skills to keenly observe and carefully learn from nature. From the teacher nature man learns many things. Therefore pedagogy starts with this.

OVERVIEW

"The Pearls of Wisdom"
Jiji Thomson
Formerly Chief Secretary of Kerala

The very first issue of Harvard Business Review, published in the fall of 1922, promised the readers what HBR would offer: "Unless we admit that rules of thumb, the limited experience of executives in each individual business, and the general sentiment of the street, are the sole possible guides for executive decisions of major importance, it is pertinent to inquire how the representative practices of business men generally may be made available as a broader foundation for such decisions, and how a proper theory of business is to be obtained."

The practices that business men adopt are not solely dependent on text books; they are governed by the nature, culture and other day to day practices. Harrington Emerson, the first management guru claimed that his ideas on management had been drawn from the study of three thoughts: the conducting of symphony orchestras, the breeding of racehorses and railway time tables.

Through a series of crisp and thought provoking editorials that the author of this book, Dr. Radhakrishnan Nair published in the SCMS Business Journal, exhorts the readers to look around and draw lessons from the nature and society. "The best management classes will be those sliced from experiences from Nature. Growth and development are all well understood from our observation of the growth and development of a plant and similar other organisms." (page 1)

This book which is a compilation of editorials penned by the author is basically a pointer: It points to the pitfalls where business executives fall when they ignore the rules of nature and culture and points to the practices that they need to adapt. "Business demands adaptation. The more it is adaptive, the more it is international. It shows that its success rests on adaptation. Adaptation here means adaptation to business culture through three groups of its manifestations: cultural imperatives, cultural electives and cultural exclusives." (page 24)

Writing on business culture, the author points out how important it is for every business house to adhere to its business culture. To take an example from the fashion industry, while rival fashion houses struggled and were acquired by conglomerates, Prada has prospered. Prada's CEO points out that it has a lot to do with the company's culture. They could remain independent in a consolidating industry. Although they had to change their plans, the way they managed the company remained constant. The values that guided their decisions, the way they organized themselves, how they communicated with one another and with their stakeholders - all remained the same. Therefore, the key to Prada's success is related to these principles. They are universal and can be successfully applied by anyone.

Frederick Taylor wrote: "the best management is a true science, resting upon clearly defined laws, rules and principles." His stated goal was: "maximum prosperity for the employer, coupled with the maximum prosperity for each employee," through "a far more equal division of the responsibility between the management and the workmen." Ever since Taylor published his *Principles of Scientific Management* in 1911, the management experts have been debating on how to balance between the "the things of production" and the "humanity of production" as Oliver Sheldon put it in 1923. It was the great management guru, Peter Drucker, who argued for applying humanistic psychology to social institutions. He laid out a vision of the corporation as a social institution in which the capacity and potential of everyone involved were to be respected. Similarly, Fritz Roethlisberger, in his masterly summation of the Hawthorne experiments, described organizations as "social systems." Management's job, he stated, was to maintain their equilibrium. This eternal truth gets resonated in the writings of Dr. Radhakrishnan, who emphasises, and rightly so, on the need for a humane approach. "A good manager," the author points out, "is someone with a facility for analysis and an even greater talent for synthesis. He is someone who knows how to treat people with respect, honesty, integrity, and trustworthiness. He is someone who knows the things which make up character." The author concludes that "management myth is not merely a myth but a must for managers to scan, chew and digest and then render into real life." With the advantage of nearly four decades of experience in Government, both in Kerala and Delhi, I can say without an iota of doubt that it's the humane approach that always yields results. It is your ability to take everyone with you that counts in the long run.

The author draws our attention to the need to strengthen Indian competitiveness in the wake of growing pressure from China and other developing countries. In this context a well defined strategy is inevitable. Developing entrepreneurship, the author points out, is a key instrument of this strategy to rejuvenate Indian innovation and competitiveness. Entrepreneurship is a driving force of economic restructuring. Successive governments, both in Kerala and Delhi, have been evolving schemes for this, but with limited amount of success. The new Government in the center is aiming to bring in one lakh crores of Rupees worth of investment in the next five years. They also want to boost the Small and Medium Enterprises (SME) to generate employment. But the question is how will we foster entrepreneurship? A few components on which we should focus more are ideas, evolving a business plan, raising capital and setting up start-ups.

The entrepreneurial education should ideally consist of two parts: the first one to cover knowledge around building blocks of entrepreneurship and the second to cover a business plan. The students need to be told how some unknown Indians like Sridhar Vembu CEO of Zoho corp, Dr. Arokiaswamy Velumani of Thyrocare, Mahesh Gupta of Kent RO systems, Kailash Katkar of Quick Heal Technologies and P C Mustafa, a coolie's son who set up a 100 crore company with just 25000 rupees, all rose up to their present, incredible level. The students need to learn how Steve Jobs, the entrepreneurial legend, famously stared Apple with co founder Steve Wozniak in 1976 after dropping from college. The tech company today has a market capitalization of $870 billion. According to Steve jobs, two things are required to build a successful company: passion and people. True, nothing in this world has truly been achieved without passion!

Like Steve Jobs, Dr. Radhakrishnan Nair vociferously pleads for passion and people. Like, Dr. Abdul Kalam, our former President, who kept on exhorting our countrymen to dream big, Dr. Radhakrishnan exhorts his readers to become good dreamers. Like "brain storming", the author argues that we need "dream storming." "Many of the ills of management education could be solved if the students are conscious of the advantages of being good dreamers too which enhance their quality to use the faculty to fancy and imagine." True, only a good dreamer can become a good manager.

The pearls of wisdom that these editorials cast are so valid and thought provoking. The simple and lucid style of this English Professor makes a lasting impression on the mind of the reader. This, indeed, is a valuable torch to all students of management.

Thiruvananthapuram
01.06.2019

FOREWORD

Kishore G. Kulkarni, Ph.D.,
Distinguished Professor of Economics, Chief Editor,
International Review of Business and Economics,
College of Business, Metropolitan State University of
Denver, Denver, CO 80217-3362.

School of Communications and Management Studies (SCMS) of Kochi in India has been running many prime academic and research institutions established by Dr. G.P.C. Nayar. Among them, SCMS Cochin School of Business is not only one of the top well-run institutions in India and in World, but it also exhibits numerous characteristics of a superior research publication hub. With the recommendation of Dr. Subramanian Swamy, I was fortunate enough to visit the SCMS Cochin School of Business two times to observe it internally and externally. One of such research activities, the School has been performing over the years, is the quarterly publication. The journal is prospering under the able leadership of its long time editor, Dr. Radhakrishnan Nair. Ever since we met about 12 years ago, Dr. Nair has impressed me, an astute thinker, a formidable philosopher, truly an amazing writer, and overall a complete leader. He has been doing the job of editorship of the journal very diligently, but more importantly he has written quarterly editorials in almost all issues of the journal. This book is a product of selected outstanding writings of Dr. Nair, and I am very delighted to see its conception and production.

Even if I have authored (co-authored) more than 12 articles in SCMS Journal of Indian Management over the years, I take a special interest in reading the editorials written by Dr. Nair in each issue of the journal. As a member of editorial advisory group, I receive all the copies of the journal on a regular basis, even if I reside in USA. This also means I get the opportunity to read and analyze all the writings of Dr. Nair that he has offered so far, including the ones that are selected to be included in this book.

I find his writing style uniquely enchanting. Almost always his arguments make a subtle philosophical point or provide an area to think about in the future. He writes very well, to the point, concise, succinct and clear. Over the years, Dr. Nair has made numerous contributions to explanation of concepts; he has made several new arguments and has contributed to our overall understanding of academic life in general. I am just lucky to be associated with him for the last decade as I have learned many tricks of the trade from him. While I wish a great success to his book endeavor, I also want to express my gratitude to him. I will cherish a copy of this book and would heartily recommend to a serious thinker to buy a copy and keep on his/her book shelf for many more years.

06.06.2019

-1-

NATURE IS THE BEST TEACHER IN MANAGEMENT

Nature has its own form. No rigid rules bind her Being: the gentle breeze, the movement of clouds, the lashing fury of storm, flower-laden trees, myriad of rain drops clinging-like crystal to the swaying blades of grass, and a spider's web, quivering like dewdrops in the morning sunlight. These beautiful moments in Nature can never be captured and channelled into rules. 'Management' exists there where Nature exists in its various manifestations.

Nature manages all things using different ways. Nature creates things and objects, sustains them, destroys them, and continues this process. Once we observe Nature, it gives us many things to learn. Nature is the greatest teacher, to poets. It is so with regard to us also when we search for the best pedagogy. The best management classes will be those sliced from experiences from Nature. Growth and development are all well understood from our observation of the growth and development of a plant or similar other organisms.

Over and above what we get from Nature as beauty and objects of beauty, we can create visual beauty with natural materials, following certain rules. Good design is universal and it demands a few basic principles. Many flower arrangers use mechanical rules to make their products pleasing and attractive, though sans creativity and soul. A thorough understanding of the basic principles of combination of flowers: Focal Point, Build-up, Balance, Relationship of Parts and Simplicity, is necessary to provide unity and harmony.

One flower in a container does not please. It has no design. Sight of two flowers, of the same height, does not please either. It is uninteresting and dull. Three flowers at different heights with the largest in the centre make a design, with the centre flower as the focal point. The focal point is the mass, prominent through shape, size or colour. Build-up is achieved by repetition of culture, form, or texture, leading to or away from the focal point. Form and colour are important factors of balance and are closely related. Relationship of parts, or proportion, or scale is necessary to obtain the best visual effect. Simplicity means finding the essence of the design.

Mass is the material, the flowers, the foliage, and the twigs used in an arrangement. Texture is the feel of the mass, rough, smooth, or delicate, and finally colour, which plays an important role. A design is the product of the three above. Similarly from the simple to the complex, lessons from Nature are many. Every object around is a provider of a lesson in pedagogy. Nature can teach us how to solve a problem. All these can form the basis of management pedagogy.

-2-

CONSERVE THE LUNGS OF OUR EARTH!

Forests are, no doubt, the lungs of the earth! They purify the air we breathe; they store carbon; and they provide free services to all life - water, soil, and oxygen! They help in maintaining global climate as well as recharge our water sources. They are therefore crucial for the survival of life on earth.

Forests are home to some of the most unique plants, birds, and animal species. They support a diversity of life forms. The flora and fauna are abundant and varied in India. They are housed in 13 biosphere reserves, 89 national parks, and more than 400 wildlife sanctuaries. The second biggest land use in the country, after farming, is forests. They encompass 67.83 millions of hectares in India. They represent 20.64 percent of the nation's geographic territory.

In spite of these abundant gifts that forests give, hundreds of acres of forests are being cleared and burned. About thirty million acres of forests are cleared globally every year! Almost fifty percent of the logging in forests is illegal. Deforestation causes twenty percent of all carbon pollution causing global climate change. Water sources are drying up and soil is lost due to erosion. Flash floods and landslides are causing loss of life. The role of our nation in reducing forests is not small.

Forests are life support systems for the rural poor offering them food, fibre and energy. The loss of forests has pushed many species to the brink of extinction.

We forget the "Forest Principles" adopted by The United Nations Conference on Environment and Development in Rio in 1992 capturing international understanding in conservation of forests.

It is here we are reminded of the magic dictum: Sustainable Forest Management (SFM) plays a great role. It envisages the stewardship and use of forest lands sustaining their biodiversity, productivity, regeneration capacity, vitality, and their potential. It ensures relevant ecological, economic, and social functions, at local, national and global levels. It resolves not to cause any damage to other eco-systems.

A National Institute of Forestry alone will not suffice the needs of the nation. Every b-school has to take up, as a global requirement, the responsibility to preserve the lungs of our planet, each as a leader in the field of Forestry, Environment, and National Research Management Education so that the earth may survive, or this earth will perish.

-3-

ECOLOGY AND CULTURE

The ecological idea of culture has been predicated upon twin convictions: culture is limited to the human species and culture is the product of human creation. But, a closer and deeper study broadens our perception: culture is also concerned with nature, and with the intimate relationship between human beings and the natural environment. This revelation leads to a long leap in the idea of culture and this demands opening the doors to nature; to natural environment; and other species.

The ecological idea of culture springs out from the 'environmental movement' sweeping all over the world spreading the message that the lack of knowledge on environment will ultimately annihilate nature and exterminate the human race from the surface of this globe. We believe that economics and technology have not liberated us from our traditional dependency on the natural environment. They, instead, have increased our dependency.

Now, there is a greater awareness: natural environment provides human beings with the sustenance they need for survival and human beings owe incredible dependency to all forms of plant, animal, and mineral life. Cultures that ignore this intimate relationship between human beings and the natural environment run the risk of over extending themselves, collapsing, and disappearing from the global scene because they are unsustainable. History is full of examples of this.

Culture is also predicated on the conviction that it is the organizational form structures of different species, both human and nonhuman. It is another leap to the idea of culture. They all obey laws of nature: of birth and death, growth and decay, consumption, digestion, and elimination. Therefore we talk about the culture of plants and animals. We use phrases: wolf culture and plant culture, we use terms like horti-culture, agriculture, silvi-culture and perma-culture. The former refers to activities involving other species. The latter refers to activities involving human beings.

Everybody generally agrees with the biological idea of culture. Like human beings they also see and interpret the world. They organize themselves in groups like a flock of geese, communities like a colony of ants, as a pack of wolves, as cats basking in the sun, playing with each other. The life abiding by the well-defined systems of queen, drone, and worker bees, rigid hierarchies and divisions of labour, finely tuned communication net works, and sensing capabilities, highly evolves production, distribution, and consumption mechanisms act to ensure the survival of bees as a species and to their biological and non biological requirements, guaranteeing continuous supply of products: honey, wax, the beehive, and the honey comb; of functional and aesthetic significance. Ecology linked culture is the need of the hour.

-4-

NATURE AND HUMAN NATURE

Gloomy weather causes depression. Sunshine appears to raise the spirits. In England, the dull weather of winter drastically cuts down the amount of sunlight that is experienced. It affects some people. They become depressed. They lack in energy during the period. Their work and social life are affected. This condition is termed SAD (Seasonal Affective Disorder). Sufferers can fight back by making the most of any sunlight in winter. They can spend a few hours each day under special, full spectrum lamps. In Russia, children learn better after being exposed to ultraviolet light. In warm countries workers are allowed a siesta during the hottest part of the day.

Scientists have discovered relations between the weather and human man's moods and performance. Tempers grow shorter in hot, muggy weather. Crimes grow, rise in the summer, when the weather is hotter. Crimes fall in the winter when the weather is colder. In the US, research has established a link between temperature and street riots. The frequency of riots waxes as the weather gets warmer. Psychologists say how being cold affects performance: researchers compare divers working in icy cold water at 5°C with others at 20°C. The colder water makes the divers worse at simple arithmetic and other mental skills. Psychologists also say people become less skeptical and more optimistic when the weather is sunny.

A connection between weather and mood is made believable by the evidence for a connection between behaviour and the daylight hours. This is due to melatonin, a hormone produced in the pineal gland in the brain. The amount of melatonin falls with the greater exposure to sun light. Melatonin plays an important part in the seasonal behaviour of certain animals. A study in Belgium shows that a telephone counseling service receives more calls from people with suicidal feelings when it rains. The positive charge increases the level of serotonin, a chemical involved in sending signals in the nervous system. High levels of serotonin of the nervous system make people more active and reactive and aggressive. Mistral, the wind in Southern France and the Fohn in South Germany can affect the moods.

Melatonin, a natural hormone derivative from serotonin produced in the brain, communicates information about light to different parts of the body. It helps regulate biological rhythms and plays an important role in the reproductive cycles of many animals. It is best known for helping to regulate the body's circadian rhythm: sleep-wake cycle. Melatonin is marketed as a dietary supplement. It is touted as a cure-all for insomnia, jetlag, and even cancer and aging. Many businesses flourish on dietary supplementary products. In the UK, 400,000 ionizers are sold every year. These small machines raise the number of ions in the air in a room. Many people claim that they feel better in negatively charged air.

There is a threat to Nature from man's urge for development at the expense of Nature. Moreover, as Nature is being unscrupulously exploited, the rhythm nature maintains suffers changes. All these have upset the equilibrium of Nature and consequently that of human mind. Ultimately these will upset the apple cart of man's designs to live a life of peace, prosperity and harmony.

It is our duty to protect and preserve Nature to sustain the human life on earth.

-5-
MANAGE THE MANNA WE GET FROM THE MOTHER EARTH

"Drip, dribble, trickle, and drizzle." Don't you hear the "splash" sounds? They are the sounds of water.

Water is one of the commonest substances in the universe. Water wraps the planet. But ninety percent of water so available is salty. Much of the rest is locked up in ice. The human ingenuity and passions demand an adequate supply of water. It has been the prize in conflicts around the world.

Even in the century ahead, we cannot boast to procure and conserve adequate water to satisfy the increasing demand. Despite our progress, half of the world's population till suffers with water services inferior to those available to the ancient Greeks and Romans.

Local mismatches between demand and supply could push groups to violence, retard economic progress, and devastate populations.

Pure water marks off heaven from Hell. Future days are not too far off for us to think that the place bestowed with water is the place blessed with sanctity. God of water will be the power centre in the near future. Human life on earth will be hydrocentric. Water god will be the chief among deities.

We drink it. We generate energy from it. We soak our crop with it. We have stretched our supplies to the breaking point. Do we have enough clean water to fulfill our water requirement?

If we invoke the Purana to justify our argument that a war between the demons and gods took place for manna, we can well hope that a similar scene will be re-enacted soon for the sake of pure water as the scanty availability of this life sustaining liquid will make it manna. Myths, legends and written histories reveal repeated controversy over fresh water sources since ancient times. Scrolls from Mesopotamia indicate that the states Umma and Lagesh in the Middle East clashed over the control of irrigation canal some 4,500 years ago.

As the world's population continues to grow, dams, aqueducts and other kinds of infrastructure will have to be built in countries where basic needs have not been met. The fastest and cheapest solution is to expand the productive and efficient use of water. In many countries, more than thirty percent water never reaches the intended destinations owing to the leaky pipes, faulty equipment, and properly maintained distributive system.

Business shall turn its focus on Man's Basic Needs including tapping and generating Water. Management shall take up the tasks to preserve Water to sustain the life of all the living.

–6–

BUSINESS AND CLIMATE CHANGE

An ontological enquiry into business will lead to many revelations, of which one is: business exists physically on earth. Spatially, the earth thereby emerges as the subject of study in business. The earth is a source of resources for business. Man taps the perennial resources of the earth. Are they really perennial? These "perennial" resources are under severe threats. Among them the climate change is one, though this had been taken for granted by man for a long time. It's high time we took up the causes of climate change and its after-effects on human life, as the subject of study and research. This can help us evade them in the days to come.

Alarm bells ring. People still deem it a false alarm. They don't lend their ears to the calls of scientists forewarning them of imminent havoc to befall them if they ignore the phenomenon, climate change.

What is surprising is that, though late, interest in climate change at length is noted in developed countries as a corrective strategy, in developing countries an agonizing reality and in under-developed countries, a frightening daydream. The climate has always been changing. Past changes, etched on the landscape, have influenced the evolution of all life forms. Past changes are the subtext of our economic and social history. Current changes form the centre of the debate about the consequences of human activities on the global environment especially in developing countries.

There are two principal reasons for this development. It was not until the work of a few dedicated researchers such as Hubert Lamb in England and J. Murray Mitchell in the USA, in the 1950s and 1960s, that the reality of recent climate change became an accepted scientific concept. The second reason for increased interest has been the growing realization during the last few decades that recent climate changes may well be, at least mostly, the result of human activities. Over and above these, an essential component of climate studies has been the explosive growth of computer technology.

Business can survive only if resources are aplenty. The earth is the resource provider. Only when man disturbs the equilibrium of earth, it invokes destruction. For the well-being of the living beings on earth, the space for business, climate-related matters shall be given maximum concern aided by the know-how of the scientists. Our Journal welcomes articles from intelligentsia on the subject.

-7-

CULTURE AND BUSINESS

Culture is a word, semantically a hard nut to crack. It's more so in the present context, may be because of the convergence of interests of the earlier kinds of its meanings.

Culture is a complex term. It is a noun of process: culture refers to (cultivation) of crops, or (rearing and breeding) of animals. By extension of meaning, culture lifts us off to the culture (active cultivation) of the human mind. Culture in the course of time has become a noun of configuration or generalization of the spirit which informs the whole way of life of a distinct people. In the 19th century, Herder (1784-91) first used "cultures" in deliberate distinction from any singular. We use it for linear sense of civilization. Culture designates a whole and distinctive way of life. It raises certain fundamental questions. It is the nature of the formative/determining elements which produce culture. There has been a strong development of the sense of culture as the active cultivation of the mind.

Culture until recently was neglected by sociologists. But it is now the subject of lively and controversial discussions in most of the fields of activities, even in the sphere of business.

Culture evoked a developed state of mind - as in the usage "a person of culture." It underwent a change to mean the process of this development as in the "cultural interests" and "cultural activities." From this sense, it changed into the means of these processes as in culture as the "acts" the human intellectual works, the one rated as the most common accepted theory.

There are two main kinds of culture: a) giving emphasis of an 'informing' spirit of a whole way of life manifest over the whole range of social activities: language, styles of art, and various kinds of intellectual work, and b) giving accent on a whole social order in which a specifiable culture in styles, art and kinds of intellectual work, seen as the product of a social order. These positions are classified into: Idealist and Materialist. Both these positions are undergoing changes as business that has crept into the concept of institutions, formations, means of production, identifications, forms, reproduction, and organization of culture has totally changed human life.

In a rapidly expanding global marketplace, it is crucial to understand the economic benefits cultural awareness can bring into the world of business.

-8-

BUSINESS CULTURE

Culture has evolved as an idea spanning over two thousand years. Culture as a reality has existed for a far longer period. It came into existence as the Romans used the term 'cultura' to mean cultivation in classical times making it one of humanity's oldest ideas. Since then, many ideas of culture have been advanced and adopted. Among them are:way of life, cultivation, the arts and humanities, the legacy from the past, heritage of mankind, a complex whole or total way of life, values, beliefs and behavior, the relationship between beings and the environment, and the organizational forms and structures of different species. Most of them boil down to two things: Culture is helping people to understand the world and many different things that exist in the world; and helping people to change the world in order to improve their own situations, the human condition, or the world at large. For this, it has been necessary to enlarge the idea of culture progressively over the centuries, from culture as cultivation, popular in classical times, to culture as the organizational forms and structures of different species, increasingly popular today.

In language, this word culture claims the greatest flexibility, adaptability, and versatility when it is understood in these terms. As most ideas are static and unchanging, culture is dynamic and evolutionary. It has been in tune with the rapidly changing nature of reality and human knowledge and understanding. It has now an all - encompassing idea. Taking our cue from this, culture is defined as "the way in which species in general - and the human species in particular -create wholes or total ways of life that are composed of many different parts as they go about the process of meeting their individual and collective needs and working out their complete association with the world."

Culture is of much importance to the world. On the one hand, it embraces virtually everything that exists in the world. On the other hand, it affirms the fact that the world is made up of culture in general and countless cultures in particular at its very core and essence. Economics and economies constitute an extremely important part of this because they are concerned with the creation of material and monetary wealth with people's jobs, income, and sources of livelihood. They form part and parcel of a substantially broader, deeper, and more fundamental process in present day culture: developing a new business culture that is going to rein supreme, setting the real foundation of existence and survival of nature and human beings.

–9–

CULTURE AND ADAPTATION: IMPERATIVES, ELECTIVES, AND EXCLUSIVES

Cultural adaptation is a golden phrase in business. It does not connote one has to do away with one's own culture to adapt to another. Of course one has to adhere to some cultural beliefs religiously. One has to know what one can abstain from too. Moreover, one has to be surely discreet in what one has to agree to some beliefs under specific situations.

Some companies show apathy towards adaptation. They think they are superior to others. Therefore they will not budge from their culture. They are reluctant to that. They think that it's others who have to adapt to their culture. Cultural imperialism doesn't let a culture adapt itself to other so called subservient cultures. One telling example is business organizations despite their initial prejudices for their native tongue, have successfully accepted English culture through the language in their communication activities.

Business demands adaptation. The more it is adaptive, the more it is international. It shows that its success rests on its adaptation. Adaptation here means adaptation to business culture through three groups of its manifestations: cultural imperatives, cultural electives, and cultural exclusives.

Cultural imperatives are customs that we must conform to if we wish to ensure success in business. Building relationships is an offshoot of cultural Imperative. Relationship management is now a common phrase. In China and Japan it is used meticulously. Business people do not business with companies. They do it with people. As we launch business in another country, the cultural imperative demands spending time building relationship there. Never shall we underestimate the relevance of building trust with your business partner. It will break or make a deal.

Cultural electives are customs we have to conform to, but there is no compulsory conformation demanded. We may be uncomfortable with many customs and beliefs in other countries. But we may politely decline what we don't solicit. In the Czech Republic it is said liquor is offered to break the ice at b-meetings. Time is not a factor. To friendship and trust, it is mandatory even in the dawn. You can politely accept the offer, you can have a ceremonial sip, or you pretend you sip. Arabs offer coffee to sign friendship. You are expected to accept it. It doesn't mean you need drink it. Most such customs fall under the cultural elective category.

Cultural exclusives are customs that are meant for locals only. We will even break a deal if we partake in these customs. A Christian in Middle East shall not act like a Muslim, which is deemed an insult to Islam. Never crack a joke on another country's politics. Never speak critically or skeptically on another's custom. We have to be very strict in dealing cultural exclusives.

-10-

CRICKET/BUSINESS: UNDERSTANDING CULTURE

There are many ways to understand culture from cultural studies. The cultural studies explore the meanings of every day processes, places, and acts like communications, space, and shopping. In this process, new meanings are manufactured. An ideology is being coded into everyday life. The emphasis here is on the business of cricket, which has become part of everyday life. Cricket is a text/system of meanings. An attempt is made to understand culture from the point of view that cricket is business.

Cricket is a sports event. It is a system of meanings. It is a text. There is a formal arrangement of players, infrastructure: wickets, boundary markers, crease lines on the pitch, and other people. We separate the players from (1) the umpire, (2) the audience/spectators. We separate the players among themselves: batsmen, bowlers, fielders, and wicket keeper. We identify the players as belonging to two distinct sides. We identify the processes of the game: bowling, batting, fielding and the rules that they follow. We note the arrangement of the players in particular locations. The movement along the processes of the game is important: one side bats, the other bowls and fields, the umpires referee. Then after one side is bowled out, the other bats and tries to exceed the total number of runs raised by the first side. This is the progression of events within the context of the game.

All these constitute the text of the game; where meaning (winner/loser) is decided through the process of difference, logical movement and our understanding of what is going on out there in the field. Remember, the meaning generated depends on our understanding of the rules: the language formula and structure and sequence of what is happening. Thus the text of a cricket match may be analyzed at three levels: 1) It is a system in itself with its own constitutive elements and laws (the grammar of player arrangements and its rules). 2) It is one element in the sporting system as a whole. That is the generic contexts of a cricket match within the system of other sports, its difference from football and its rules. 3) It relates to culture as a whole (the Indian obsession with cricket and the money involved).

Cricket has generated an obsession among Indians. The charm of the game leads to profit maximization. Money flows into cricket match ticket selling counters. Slowly cricket metamorphoses into a charm. Profit, the purpose of business, of course, is the objective condition of economic activity. Cricket match attracts huge crowds. Stadiums change to venues of product sales, of all items ranging from food items to fancy items. It turns out to be a place of entrepreneurial function: marketing and innovation. Cricket becomes instrumental to infrastructure development. Cricket players become corporate ambassadors. Cricket initially turns out to be a symbol, an index, and finally becomes an icon of business. All these have led cricket to become a power centre, the focus of cultural studies.

-11-

B TECHNO CULTURE AND RISK

Contemporary critical theory negotiates with massive environment disaster, industrial disaster, and other cataclysmic events. Contemporary social theory examines the role of such events play in culture. One of the most influential of such theories is that of the risk society.

In the book, *Risk Society: Towards a New Modernity*, Ulrich Beck propounded the thesis: risk society. To him risk is not real. Risks are about 'becoming real.' As soon as risk becomes real, it becomes disaster. Risk then gets displaced to other 'sites:' future disasters. So, risks are potential disasters. A domain where risk thesis is relevant is techno-culture. We live in a technological world. Global capitalism runs on the engines of information and communications technologies. Our everyday life depends on technology and is vulnerable to technological threats. Beck begins by suggesting that techno-science in industrial society has generated numerous dangers. Industrial society is based on the production and distribution of goods-required to fill the 'scarcity' within society. Beck suggests that a society based on scarcity and removal of scarcity can handle goods and needs only when they actualize as visible. Such a system cannot handle the risks and hazards of industrial production and distribution. But as long as risk is secondary to scarcity or needs industrial society has no problems. This is the feature of industrial modernity. In other words, risk generates solutions which generate more risks. Individualized beings experience newer forms of insecurity and anxieties. We have here a culture of warnings in banks, railway coaches, and malls. Anyway you go and you discover warnings against all kinds of dangers and risks. This has something to do with excessive technological, technologised and mediated information made available to us. With increasing and easier access to information and the risk of releasing confidential information-Credit cards members and residential address by children via the internet-have both increased risk considerably. When techno-science reveals the risk involved in contamination and other newer problems previously unknown, it also delivers information about these risks. It produces risks by making us aware of these risks. Beck's solution to the autopoietic risk culture is to find political potential outside government.

-12-

SENSE OF TOUCH AND BUSINESS

Every sense is associated with an organ of our body: sight with the eye, sound with the ear, taste with the tongue, and smell with the nose. There is a fifth one too, the sense of touch, difficult to explain along these lines. The studies in psychology and physiology show that touch has direct and crucial effects on the growth of the body and the mind. Touch is a means of communication so critical that its absence retards growth in infants, owing to the neuro-chemical effects of skin-to-skin contact. Certain brain chemicals released by touch, or others released in its absence, may account for the infant's failure to thrive. The studies are relevant against a backdrop of continuing research on the psychological benefits of touch for emotional development.

In business, touch is important in many products and services. It can be a direct experience with a product. It can be about the contact with our skin. Touch and its implications on customer behaviour or the importance of touching products during buying process and the lack of it in non-touch-media like e-commerce and mail order have been researched. The purpose is the effect of tactile sense, visual sense and order of simulation on the product attitude. The purpose is the effect of product attitude of utilitarian product and hedonstic product individually.

A lot of research has been done on the haptic aspects of touch. This kind of work has been classified into four categories. The first category of experiments is used to test the quality of fabric and the order of simulation by controlling the experiment environment and the affecting time, the main material of this experiment being fabric. The second refers to the difference noted between touchable product and untouchable product, to control different information and the literature description on the product, the main materials of this experiment being brooms and diamonds. The general research findings are as follows: i) the effect of tactile sense, vision and order of simulation and the product attitudes are significant, ii) the effect of order of simulation matched by tactile sense on the product attitude is significant, and iii) the effect of order of simulation matched by vision on the product attitude is not significant. The third category is about utilitarian product, providing rational written description as better than perceptual written description. The fourth one is about hedonistic product, providing perceptual written description as better than rational written description. The creation of a full sensory and emotional experience for the customer can open marketing opportunities in the future, but there has been little research work done carried out in recent years on the potential of cutaneous perception as a marketing tool. Haptics, the branch of psychology that investigates cutaneous sense data, has the potential to open up many avenues in business. Haptics, as the science of integrating the sense of touch into human/computer interactions, promises to greatly expand the reach of computer into everyday life. "Someday soon, drivers will be alerted by a little tap on their shoulder when another car is riding in their blind spot." Two business applications for haptics are virtual reality (including games and medical training) and remote operation (teleoperation). Haptics allows users to touch and feel objects in CAD/CAM and similar systems.

The tactile sense will reign supreme in inventions and innovations in the realm of business and industry in the days to come and it will be an integrating force in organizational culture.

-13-

THE EAR AND BUSINESS

The sensory organ of the auditory system is the ear. Sound waves cause the tympanic membrane (ear-drum) to vibrate and humans can hear sounds: waves with frequencies between 20 and 20,000 Hz. This faculty of the ear is greatly related to business today.

Consumer spending on music is noted in three sectors: recorded music, live music, and music instruments. Recorded music dominates, but this large market is on the cusp of a technological revolution that will eventually transform the way the majority of people buy music. By 2010 legal down loading will account for more than a third of consumer spending on recorded music. In mainstream music, recording and marketing are now dominated by just four majors worldwide: UK's EMI Group PLC, Universal Group and Warner Music Group (US), and SONY BMG (Japan/Germany). The world of music provides an excellent metaphor for today's business climate: by examining the orchestra and the conductor, the jazz band and improvisation, the composer and innovation, music and management, it introduces a dynamic vocabulary for discussing leadership, teamwork, creativity and personal development, inviting participants to explore new ways of thinking about business practice.

Every business is becoming a "music business" or, more accurately, an entertainment business. Tom Peters claims that it's barely an exaggeration to say that everyone is getting into the entertainment business. Music Business to Musician Business taking a cue from the cyber-bard John Perry Barlow, we could see a paradigm shift from the domination of the music business to that of the musician business. What do the cultural industries do? The cultural industries, the recording industry, the arts, television, and radio commodify, package, and market experiences as opposed to physical products or services. Their 'stock in trade' is selling on short term access to simulated worlds and altered states of consciousness. The fact is that they are an ideal organizational model for a global economy that is metamorphosing from commodifying goods and services to commodifying cultural experience itself. The same forces that are undoing the larger business companies are empowering individual musicians. As a result, the idea of a music career is sprouting new wings as artists and industry careerists begin discarding intoxicating myths and tapping into some new-found powers. The triune Music Industries develop side by side: the mainstream pop/rock business, will continue to market established stars like Celine Dion and Whitney Houston, the chaotic illegal record business will involve pirates and bootleggers, and the indie, genre music scenes (local players connected through websites and digital radio, but commercial in their niche) will make enough money to go on making music.

Music may be defined romantically as the food of love (Shakespeare). Music, in prosaic business terms, is sound with particular characteristics. However, it is undeniably a vibrant art form and one which touches more people, in more ways than any other art form.

In business, music certainly generates a higher market value than the other arts, although a comprehensive market size for music in all its manifestations is impossible to calculate.

-14-

SMELL AND MANAGEMENT

The sense of smell is critical for all: for finding food, for avoiding predators, or for choosing mates. We can distinguish over ten thousand different odour molecules. Smell/odour is perfume/fragrance when it is pleasant. It's stench/repugnant when it is unpleasant. We utilize our sense of smell to enjoy the aroma of fresh coffee, or decide the person with whom to sit next on the bus.

Every time we inhale, currents of air swirl up through the nostrils, over the bony turbinates to millions of olfactory receptor neurons. The interaction of the right molecule with the right receptor causes the receptor to change its shape (structural conformation). This change in structural conformation gives rise to an electrical signal that goes to the olfactory bulb, then to the brain that converts the electrical signal to a smell. Yes, people interact with the environment through the senses.

Smell or effluvia is considered from the chemical, physical, and physiological points of view. It is interesting to note how odours may affect cognitive performance. In business, the idea that the sense of smell can have strong effects on consumer responses to retail environments is well made use of. The claims, that the odours have strong persuasive powers, tantalize retailers looking for the competitive edge. A lot of retailing relevant olfaction research is going on throughout the world.

Some Software company one day may announce a radical breakthrough in Computer Scent Technology. The Internet will come to its "senses." Now, you can already chat, email, download music and watch video through the internet, but imagine you are able to smell fresh seaside air from the heart of the city, or savour the smell of your favourite restaurant's cuisine while booking a table. Digital Scent Technology can also change the interactive entertainment experience to movies, games, music, animation, or any digital media.

Anthropology of odour has been instrumental to establishment of many industries. It's interesting to learn how cultures rely on fragrance for healing, communication and hunting. The effect of odoriferous plants on the annual economy of nations is a subject matter worth study. The scent of lavender and jasmine enhance sleep. Earlier studies investigating the effects of aroma on sleep found a tendency for the scents to disrupt sleep. It can contribute to enjoyment of life through the perception of pleasant odours such as perfume, food and flowers.

Flavour and fragrance industry leaders have "telling" tales of over 175 industries on the prospects in the field. The cosmetic/beauty store industry comprises 10,000 stores with combined annual income of about $7 million. The industry is labour-intensive with average annual revenue per worker being $85000. Stenchy trash can also become crowning resource for industry. Trafficking in toxic waste is also another area of interest of the world. Products of environmental solutions for chemically-free water treatments, air-conditioners, water conditioners and water softeners are of high demand in the markets. Anyhow "Smell" will open up umpteen avenues for business activities.

-15-

TASTE AND MANAGEMENT

The concept of taste cannot now be separated from the concept of consumer. "Taste" and "good taste" have got themselves separated from active human senses and have become much a matter of acquiring certain habits and rules, in spite of its ironic relation to the actual history of the word.

The word "taste" has been in English since 13 century A.D. In the beginning it meant 'wider than our taste.' It was rather similar to our touch or feel. It created a tactile experience. The 14 century A.D. narrowed its range down and brought it closer to the mouth reducing it to a mere gustatory experience. "Good taste" in the sense of "good understanding" has been recorded from 1425 A.D. and in the sense of "spiritual taste," since 1502. Taste later in 1784 A.D. turned into a synonym for discrimination: "that quick discerning faculty or power of the mind by which we accurately distinguish the good, bad or indifferent."

Gradually, "tasteful" and "tasteless" grew to mean and suggest ideas and concepts of various proportions, permutations and combinations. Taste metamorphosed into a metaphor, taken from a passive sense of the human body and then transferred to things - which in their essence not passive - to intellectual acts and operations.

Business world christened the word "taste" and adopted it into its realm. It is now a powerful addition into business diction. A plethora of applications of taste we note in business. When you are buying or ordering a bottle of Chivas Regal, the natural thing is to mentally visualize how it's going to taste. In Taste events, taste understands that effective management is achieved by meticulous planning and co-ordination through operational detail and clear communication. A taste of Restaurant Management, diverse, exciting and fast-paced, does not restrict itself to mere culinary control but it transcends to the restaurant industry. Design Print Media have formally been re-branded. It has become Taste Media.

Business uses necromancy to conjure up consumers 'out of the void' using the potent wand of brand, induces taste in the consumer for the product , then sells it addressing the consumer prince/princess or king/queen, and satiates its desire for profit to the full. Even the taste of the consumer, sometimes, is also a product generated out of the clever and crafty machinations in business. Through branding, advertising and taste building, the product is introduced and launched into the market by the producers. The two ideas: the tactile taste and the business taste in modern times have been developing together responding to aesthetic and business demands affected by the conception that the viewer or reader is a consumer, exercising and subsequently showing certain level of taste. As a company fulfils its desired target on the very first day of the launch of its product, it's getting a real taste of success. Changing workplaces in a corporate may not be to everybody's taste.

"Taste and management" deserves attention from the promoters of b-education and research as food industry grooms itself to be the largest industry in the world with its challenges in the fields of producing, processing and marketing.

-16-

COLOUR AND MANAGEMENT

The concept of 'colour' is simple. However, it conjures up different ideas for each of us. The physicist conceives colour as determined by the wavelength of light. The physiologist and the psychologist presume that our perception of colour involves neural responses to the eye and the brain. Colour is not only a thing of beauty, but also a determinant of survival in nature, so says the naturalist. The social historian and the linguist believe that our understanding and interpretation of colour are inextricably linked to our own culture. In the eyes of the painter, colour provides a means of expressing feelings and the intangible, making possible the creation of a work of art.

The state of the art in management research conforms itself to research in Finance/Marketing/HR/Operation. It's restrictive owing to its accent on job potential and employment. Research, here, is also limited to the restricted compass. It's high time management research got relieved of the trodden track of this research trajectory. Once an attempt is made to evaluate management research, we will be startled to learn that valid and fruitful research is yet to be made on basic issues in management like its "nature" and its "function." Hitherto only empirical research has been encouraged. It's in this context that we wish if we could take up research with perception through senses, fundamental to comprehension. Introspection on how the eye (visual sense of perception) has been properly used in managerial comprehension is interesting to note. Therefore, it's suggested that three phases of research in this area are worth exploring: 'management' in colour, 'colour' in management and 'colour' and 'management.'

Once we love to learn and understand the manifold aspects of colour, we must swing between the hard sciences and the fine arts. It's interesting to note the continuous shift between 'two cultures,' which give an impression that they are antithetical to each other. In the field of colour, however, the arts and sciences travel in unison, and together they provide rich and comprehensive understanding of the subject. Management is an area of knowledge that defies any reduction of the field into either art or science. It is highly interdisciplinary. It's vivid and spectacular like a painting, with contributory blending in like individual colours to form a unique piece of art.

-17-

DREAM-STREAMING

Dreams form a powerful alternative source of consciousness. Consciousness leads us to realms of being and imagination. Unless we integrate dreams into our lives, we can never use this most potential resource for personal and collective change. Access to dreams demands to pay no fee. Nor it requires remitting tax. It's absolutely free of cost or tax. It's true to aerobics too. But it necessitates exerting physical energy. It makes your forehead to glisten with drops of sweat. It compels your joints to bear ache for even certain yoga postures.

 We needn't wear any uniform. We can just wear a casual, or even birthday suit, to practise experiencing dreams. Pay attention to the dreams that visit us, repeatedly throughout each night. Just we need to show willingness to consider the possible messages they convey. As we read this, the director, producer, casting manager, and composers are hard at work creating the late night show staged for you, exclusively tonight.

 If we wake up during the night / in the morning, we won't open our eyes wide open. We will lie still. We will try gently to recall any imagery present, as we are awake.

If we successfully recall any specific image, we will try to connect it with whatever activity that preceded it. And what preceded even that and what had preceded it, tracing it as back as we can. Once we have recreated them, we will rehearse them a few times, before opening our eyes. Record them in the reverse order. Describe the dream fully to yourself. When you try later, how you write initially may have more significance.

We can look for similarities, yes, between what we experienced in our dream and in our waking life. Were things in our dreams distorted? We will examine puzzling images in our dreams. Let's use the techniques of free association (Freud), amplification (Jung), or dialoguing (Gestalt) to explain our writing.

We know managers shall be good dreamers. They shall make use of all our untapped resources of brain and mind to manage men, machines and money. Dreams change man and manager. Once we make up our mind, we will start our preparation today. We get a suitable notebook/diary. We place it under pillow lest we should forget. We will record the dreams, tomorrow early in the dawn. As soon as we get into the bed, we will review the experiences of the day. Let us pay particular attention to any unresolved emotion that stirred us up. We will have to relax as fully as possible. We need to petition our inner source of dream enlightenment to provide us with dreams tonight.

-18-

DREAM-STORMING

We're all familiar with the concept of brainstorming. We're also familiar with letting ideas, thoughts, and images roam freely with the hope that they may lead to some new solution to a difficult question or problem or new thinking.

Have we ever thought of the possibilities of "dream-storming?"

Our dreaming mind has an uncanny ability to sort through a large number of details. It processes material in a way that's not limited by the usual roles of logic. Thereby, very novel and innovative suggestions are generated. When we're frustrated by a problem in our waking lives, we may find ourselves in a rut. We may go forth and back across the same familiar but unproductive ground.

In dreams, it seems we can almost hover, like a humming bird, or fly back and forth, up and down, or sideways, in order to see the problem that is stalemating us from a new angle or perspective.

A plethora of examples are provided to document the significant changes that have occurred in the worlds of art, music, drama, literature, films, architecture, politics, military conquest, athletic performance, scientific discovery, and religion because somebody acted upon inspirational imagery revealed in a vivid dream. But it is not very much so in the world of business and management.

It is interesting to learn how our ancestors experienced dreams. Dreams have been revered, feared, and puzzled ever since the dawn of history. Dreams were of different dimensions to different kinds of people. It is also challenging to know the prominent place dreams held in the nineteenth century before Freud "discovered" them.

It is a puzzling dilemma to know whether "reality" is better glimpsed with open eyes during daylight hours or with closed eyes while dreaming.

Dream imagery has the potential to serve as a "mental X-ray" allowing diagnosis of an impending physical problem before it shows up with full blown, obvious symptoms in the waking of life. There are factors that influence dreams, both physiologically and psychologically. How dreams are currently evaluated by means of EEG (brainwave monitoring) technology. How scientists tabulate the elements found in dreams to discover the patterns of dream content that exist for an individual or a particular class of dreamers?

Data are presented to show how dreams change as we age, how the dreams of men and women are different, and how stress can influence the outcome of the dreams. There is a kind of dream called lucid dreams in which the dreamer is consciously aware of participating in a dream. Repetition of these experiences can often lead to enhanced feelings of freedom, self-confidence, and rapture and cause dreamers to examine metaphysical questions with a seriousness and urgency that, for many people, may be surprising and without personal precedent.

Many of the ills in management education could be solved if the students are conscious of the advantages of being good dreamers too which enhance their quality to use the faculty to fancy and imagine.

Be good dreamers and be good managers.

-19-

WORKING WITH OUR DREAMS

Dreams have fascinated man and mankind. Socrates (c. fourth Century B. C.) puts forth the question: "What proof could you give if anyone should ask us now, at the present moment, whether we are asleep and our thoughts are a dream, or we are awake and talking to each other in a waking condition?" Theaetetus failed to offer in response proof that they were awake. He acknowledged that they could both be dreaming. Dreams are a powerful alternative state of consciousness. This state gives us access to realms of being and imagination available in no other way. Dreams are our most potent natural resource. We have to integrate dreams into our lives. We need to pay attention to the dreams given to us and consider the messages they convey.

The distinction between reality and illusion is questioned continuously in Lewis Carroll's famous book, Through the Looking Glass. Gerald Bullett, an English novelist, seemed to enjoy the enrichment provided by being a resident of both the waking and the dreaming worlds. In Bullett's essay he provides other interesting metaphors for those two domains of existence referring to "two self-contained rooms with the swing door called sleeping - and —waking, waking-and sleeping, pivoted between them."

The philosopher Schopenhauer emphasized the equivalence of our dreaming and waking states. He wrote that "life and dreams are leaves of the same book" and contended that there was no clear distinction between their natures. D.H.Laurence confessed: "I can never decide whether my dreams are the result of my thoughts or my thoughts the results of my dreams."

A consensus exists among the authors mentioned above. Crossing the threshold from the waking state to the dreaming state enriches our sensory imagery and empowers our creative capacity. Travelers passing through the "portals of sleep" arrive in a wondrous land where crystal palaces gleam, enchanting music plays, and they are endowed with wizard-like power to solve the vexation riddles that were unsolvable in their limited waking world. There is something unique about our dreaming mind that deserves greater recognition.

−20−

THE "CAVE IMAGE" AND LEARNING

The Allegory of the cave is a chapter in the Greek Philosopher Plato's The Republic. It's taken from a fictional dialogue between Plato's mentor, Socrates and Plato's brother, Glaucon. It is used to illustrate our nature in its education and want of education. The physical world is in the form of a cave. Human beings are trapped inside the cave from the beginning of life. They are stationary. They cannot move their heads. They perceive only shadows and sounds. If one of them is released and is encouraged to travel upward to the entrance of the cave! There the light may pain the eye that's accustomed to the dark. He is exposed to daylight. The world of day light represents the realm of ideas. His eyes grow slowly accustomed to this light. Gradually, he can look up to the sun. He can understand what the ultimate source of light and life is. This gradual process is a metaphor of education and enlightenment.

Plato's parable "cave image" leads to the concept of ideal education. What is expected of a good student is like that of a prisoner in the cave who breaks the shackles and reaches the opening of the cave to see the outside world. The source of light in the cave is a burning fire behind them. Those in the cave see only the light against the far wall of the cave. There are several people who play puppets in front of the fire, yet behind the prisoners. This projects shadows on to the far wall. The prisoners assume that these shadows are real, as they cannot see the fire, the puppets, or the puppeteers. Who are the prisoners? Who are the puppeteers? What are these puppets? The prisoners are those who have desire to know reality, but they don't have the will to come to light. The shadows of puppets and puppeteers give us an illusion of reality. The puppeteers make these puppets sing and dance and move to the tunes of the puppeteers. But they are not visible to the prisoners. The insiders, the prisoners, are trapped by circumstance, ignorant to a great deal of the happenings. The Cave, as we see the image, is not real at all, yet it is believed to be so by the prisoners. The fire continuously burning behind them is the urge for knowledge.

–21–

TO THINK CRITICALLY IS TO REASON CLEARLY

Critical thinking and its expression as oral and written communication, are important skills required for business graduates in their careers, say executives. Faculties in b-schools vouchsafe this. Recruiters agree with executives and faculties. B Schools stake out this territory and introduce remedial components to reinforce b-courses.

MBAs who can think about problems and articulate solutions logically are preferred by recruiters.

Universally Universities accepted the above views and initiated steps to start courses to achieve this goal. Stanford's Critical Analytical Thinking (CAT), Yale's Problem Framing Course (PFC), and Washington University's Critical thinking for Leaders (CTL) are some of these courses.

Stanford's CAT is a form of disciplined analysis. Critical thinking here focuses on the thinking and reasoning processes that underlie analysis and inquiry. The CAT has a vision to improve students' reasoning and argument building skills, while helping them to read and listen carefully. The CAT develops these skills by helping students to think about causal inference, ask the right questions, be more critical, work out the logic behind an argument, and uncover assumptions. The CAT employs a small group, seminar style format. The Course comprises seven weekly cycles. Each week students write a three page paper of one thousand words by Wednesday. Professors grade the papers and return them with comments on Friday. Writing coaches review the papers, offering detailed advice on everything from structure to pronunciation. Review by the writing coaches is mandatory for the first several weeks. It is optional later. The seminar groups meet on Thursday evening or Friday to discuss the topic on which students have written. Each week, the CAT builds different reasoning skills in the context of a single substantive topic. Throughout the course, students analyze, write about, and debate fundamental questions and phenomena that arise in many business and non-business settings.

To sum up, courses such as the CAT, the PFC, and the CTL help students practise the skills of oral and written communication that executives and recruiters found lacking in MBAs graduates.

-22-

MANAGEMENT: ONTOLOGY AND PEDAGOGY

Nature has its own form. No rigid rules bind her Being: the gentle breeze, the movement of clouds, the lashing fury of storm, flower-laden trees, myriad of rain drops clinging-like crystal to the swaying blades of grass, and a spider's web, quivering like dewdrops in the morning sunlight. These beautiful moments in Nature can never be captured and channeled into rules. 'Management' exists there where Nature exists in its various manifestations.

Nature manages all things using different ways. Nature creates things and objects, sustains them, destroys them, and continues this process. Once we observe Nature, it gives us many things to learn. Nature is the greatest teacher, to poets. It is so with regard to us also when we search for the best pedagogy. The best management classes will be those sliced from experiences from Nature. Growth and development are all well understood from our observation of the growth and development of a plant or similar other organisms.

Over and above what we get from Nature as beauty and objects of beauty, we can create visual beauty with natural materials, following certain rules. Good design is universal and it demands a few basic principles. Many flower arrangers use mechanical rules to make their products pleasing and attractive, but, sans creativity and soul. A thorough understanding of the basic principles of combination of flowers: Focal Point, Build-up, Balance, Relationship of Parts and Simplicity, is necessary to provide unity and harmony.

One flower in a container does not please. It has no design. Sight of two flowers, of the same height, does not please either. It is uninteresting and dull. Three flowers at different heights with the largest in the centre make a design, with the centre flower as the focal point. The focal point is the mass, prominent through shape, size or colour. Build-up is achieved by repetition of culture, form, or texture, leading to or away from the focal point. Form and colour are important factors of balance and are closely related. Relationship of parts or proportion or scale is necessary to obtain the best visual effect. Simplicity means finding the essence of the design.

Mass is the material, the flowers, the foliage, and the twigs used in an arrangement. Texture is the feel of the mass, rough, smooth, or delicate, and finally colour, which plays an important role. A design is the product of the three above. Similarly from the simple to the complex, lessons from Nature are many. Every object around is a provider of a lesson in pedagogy. Nature can teach us how to solve a problem. All these can form the basis of management pedagogy.

-23-

TEACHING AND LEARNING

We in India have developed a system of teaching and learning faithfully abiding by the precepts followed in the west. This is more so in the modern areas of learning like management studies. Perhaps, rather than conveniently forgetting the enlightened system that was in existence, we should have focused more on that time-old, time-tested holistic approach to teaching and learning. Our higher education field has been profusely growing quantitatively, not qualitatively. In the appendix to the Book, Eckhart Tolle and Sri Aurobindo, A. S. Dalal discusses "The Three Instruments of the Teacher."

Teaching, Example, and Influence are the three instruments of the Guru. The wise teacher will not seek to impose himself or his opinions on the passive acceptance of the receptive mind. He will throw in only what is productive and sure as a seed which will grow under the divine fostering within. He will seek to awaken much more than to instruct the receptive mind. He will aim at the growth of the faculties and the experiences of the disciple by a natural process and free expansion. He will give method as an aid, as an utilizable device. It is not treated as an imperative formula or a fixed routine. He will be on his guard against any turning of the means into a limitation, against the mechanizing of process. His whole business is to awaken the divine light and set working the divine force of which he himself is only a means and an aid, a body, or a channel.

The example is more powerful than the instruction. But it is neither the example of the outward acts nor that of the personal character which is of more importance. These have their place and their utility. What will stimulate aspiration in others is the central fact of the divine inspiration within him governing his whole life and inner state, and all his activities. This is the universal and essential element. The rest belongs to individual person and circumstance. It is this dynamic realization that the Sadhaka must feel and reproduce in him according to his own nature. He need not strive after an imitation from outside which may well be sterilizing than productive of right and natural fruits.

Influence is more important than example. Influence is not the outward authority of the teacher over his disciple, but the power of his contact, of his presence of the nearness of his soul to the soul of another, infusing into it, even though in silence that which he himself is, and possesses. This is the supreme sign of the master. Can we aspire for such an ideal education system?

-24-

GOD MANAGES COSMOS

God manages cosmos. Man manages all in the cosmos as he wishes and plans. He, as the supreme head, manages home and its inmates. He, as its chief to lead, manages a firm or a factory. He, as the 'chosen ruler' on top, manages the state.

To manage anything, what one needs is a collection of different kinds of knowledge and experience. The resource for knowledge may be human relations, marketing, health, or wealth. It's three-tier in the experiential level, that the resources get altered. Knowledge is churned and churned in the mind: The managerial broodings and meditations lead to the thought, what one thinks and thinks before he manages: The raw materials are churned out into something different here, into thought, the latent state of skill in managing. The skill is manifest in the secondary stage when the thought gets changed into the word, the word to manage; it flows out of the tongue/pen. Then to the deeds, to the tertiary level: the thought gets changed into many manifestations as steps and deeds.

All these are pointers to the fact that management is skill in thought, word and deed. These all join together to form action (managerial). The action exists in language 'space' and 'time.' Management is taught in business schools. Mostly knowledge is the subject taught in schools thereby the resource material for management 'thought' (knowledge) is only discussed. How to use this resource in language — in thought, word and deed — shall also be handled in a business school. How far this is done invites questions. To generate thought, word and deed, theories will help. The West has eclipsed the East in bringing management 'thoughts' into the classroom. Many of the ancient philosophical minds of the orient are yet to see new light. They can still be pristine in the managerial scenario.

-25-

B-SCHOOL LEARNING AND TEACHING

B-school learning and teaching are both relevant in the modern context as the world is dashing towards progress and development. The main task of a b-school is to teach, train and groom a new generation of executives. Mushrooming of b-schools has helped to quantitatively solve the issue of the demand for potential executives. That's not enough. The qualitative components - teaching, training and grooming - shall also be well taken care of. For that, a well thought out management pedagogy has to be developed. The pedagogy shall give accent on 'concentration.' Concentration can be accomplished by practice and detachment.

Practice implies incessant striving. It depends on repeated efforts. A child finds it difficult to write a few words. As he grows into adolescence, he is able to write not only words but sentences effortlessly and fluently. This is possible only through practice. Great achievements in the past are the products of continuous practice. Even now every great achievement is the fruit of persistent work. How many people would have struggled persistently for every such accomplishment! There is nothing that is impossible for men of perseverance.

Detachment implies remaining aloof from all temptations and attractions while striving to fulfill a chosen aim. In order to retain interest and concern only for the work in hand, they have to remain unconcerned about everything else. This is detachment. One engaged in accomplishing something is detached from other things. A student is expected to be devoted to the task of acquiring knowledge. But if his mind is distracted by other temptations, his education will not prosper. Once the students learn there is joy and success in concentration, they will never remain idle. They will apply themselves to practise it diligently.

Ideal students absorbed in studies forget their surroundings, even their body. Young minds are like Jog Falls: a huge volume of water, gushing down from the heights of a mountain, flows down blindly and at last, having served no purpose, loses its identity in the sea. On the other hand, a dam built across its waters, which are made to flow in regulated canals with which agricultural fields get irrigated, and rich crops get harvested, can work wonders. Similarly, across the uncultured, self-willed mental - energies of the youth (spent purposelessly), a dam of discipline and restriction must be built; canals of a code of conduct must be dug, and the water of mental powers must be made to flow into the fields of education, art, literature and skilled labour. We can see then how the glorious harvest of culture flourishes!

–26–

HOMO SYMBOLIFICUS

We have to accept the fact that man is not simply Homo sapiens; he's Homo symbolificus - he is someone who makes symbols.

The business executive outlines a proposal. The novelist weaves a gripping tale. The professor labours over a monograph. The student puzzles over a term paper. The scientist reports the findings of a recent experiment. The journalist completes a story just before the deadline. The poet captures a fleeting feeling. The diarist records the events of another day.

Their tasks may vary. But each of them confronts the challenge of creating coherent ideas in the private realm of thought. Each of them maps those ideas into the private world of linguistic symbols. In composing a written text, these individuals create meaning for themselves and potentially for their readers. They engage in special form of thinking—the making of meaning—that may well define one of the most unique characteristics of our species.

Walker Percy's fanciful term Homo Symbolificus aptly underscores the centrality of meaning-making in human life. Writing, art, music, dance, and other forms of symbol creation and manipulation reveal the very human process of giving meaning to the experiences of life. Symbolization and meaning-making are essential aspects of being human.

The drive to make sense of our world is at the heart of human nature. We do this moment by moment in interpreting our daily experience. People construct personal, informal models of their experiences. These models comprise symbols that exist both in the private mental world inside one's head and in the public physical world of written texts, works of art, and artifacts of all kinds. It is through the symbols that we communicate to others that our experience is rendered meaningful.

Human cultures are the public records of our strivings to make sense of the world through symbol creation. Culture evolves continually: as new ideas are conceived, as new symbols are gestated, and as new meanings are born. Civilizations rise and fall, but the ideas and meanings that ring true, useful, and beautiful survive for future generations of humanity.

Thinking and writing are the twins of mental life. The more expressive of the twins is writing. It can offer insights into the psychology of thinking, the more reserved member of the pair. Much of what we know about thinking stems from observations of how people solve problems with clearly defined goals. The study of writing can at least broaden and deepen our understanding. Study of writing is a remarkably rich task from a methodological and empirical view point. Writing invokes typical elements of thinking.

Thinking involves a set of mental skills that create, manipulate, and communicate to others the personal symbols of mental life. In the field of business and management, thinking resulting in writing has great advantages over the other types of problem-solving, decision-making, and reasoning tasks.

-27-

BUSINESS AND MANAGEMENT: SUBJECT AND PREDICATE

Subject and *predicate* form an inseparable pair of words in grammar, a rare combination. Both are complementary terms. Their relation to each other helps us to closely and deeply know business and management, both individually and in combination.

As business is related to management, so is subject related to predicate. Business and subject have common characteristics, and management and predicate have also common characteristics. As *predicate* makes a statement about the subject so *subject* gets life. In grammar, the relation is noted as "swim" in "Fish swim." And "is an artist" in "She is an artist."

Subject "denotes the thing you are talking about or considering in a conversation, discussion, book, film etc." Business denotes the part through the predicate of business, management. Predicate is the "part of a sentence that makes a statement about the subject." Management makes a statement of what happens in business. Management is the action part of business. In the sentence "Fish swim," "swim" suggests what the subject performs. Similarly how business performs is known through the performance of business. Business is understood only through management of the business. This shows that the knowledge of subject is mandatory to predicate. Consequently, the knowledge of business is absolutely essential to management.

Business is a general concept. The concept of business generates many meanings, common and, sometimes, meaningless. Without knowing the true appropriate semantic suggestion of its being, people use it. Many such meanings formed are due to a state of misology - hatred of reason, hatred of argument, and hatred of enlightenment - on the part of the users. In this context, propriety demands a clear understanding of business, lifting the veil of misology.

We have long been aware of what we mean by business. We, who used it to think we understood it, have now become perplexed as we really try to probe its ontological position. So it is fitting that we should raise anew the question of knowing the nature/being of business. We nowadays even get perplexed in our inability to understand the expression of being. Our primary aim in business and management research shall be to work out the question of the being of business and to do so concretely. This will lead to the research on the question of the being of management also.

In mythology or in science, universe was initially sans life/spirit. The Prime mover gave it life. The prime-mover was the life-giver. The life-giver was god. Business gets life, as universe gets life. The prime mover wanted to preserve it and destroy it if necessary. So is the business as established by its prime-mover wanted to preserve it and, if necessary, destroy it, and this necessitated management. Here too, unless we know the nature/being of universe, we cannot think of managing it.

An ontological research anyhow is absolutely essential in the case of business, and also in the case of management to understand their real nature/being. The ontological research will naturally set the stage for b-learning in its right perspective followed by management learning also in its proper direction.

-28-

ON THE MOVE: EXHAUSTION TO REPLENISHMENT

Nineties marked a kind of exhaustion in getting enough personnel in business. A sudden spurt of industrial growth demanded more and more from b-schools. It turned to b-schools for their products. Products there were scanty. Demand was more, production less. To meet the requirement, remedial measures had to be taken. Supply of more and more trained personnel was the need of the hour.

This strategy for replenishment culminated in mushrooming of b-schools. Initially, the starting of IIMs and similar other institutions like SCMS was only the cue. They were exemplary for other schools to emulate. Instead, a proliferation of b-schools all over in different hues and shapes cropped up.

What happens in a b-school is alchemy. This "medieval chemical philosophy" is the appellation proper to the process. The raw materials in a b-school are graduates in arts, science, engineering, technology, and commerce. Here, the base metal is changed into gold, the precious one. Here, the base metal is changed into gold, the precious one. Otherwise, they should have continued to add to the bulk of educated unemployed. The young graduates become marketable in the process. The transmutation of base metal in alchemy is the prime function in a b-school.

However, the fine function of alchemy has not been well addressed in many b-schools. The world is dashing forward and only technology can help it on the move. Business world equipped with technology well managed could only save it. The alchemy in a b-school trims and transforms the youth to get groomed, in the preparation of the elixir of longevity of a wholesome human race. Do all the b-schools vindicate this task?

-29-

BUSINESS AND ONTOLOGY

Ontology is the subject of study in philosophy that is concerned with the nature of existence. Where does business exist? The word Business generates proliferation of ideas: Steel business, cotton business, import business, export business, textile business, and ever so many kinds of businesses. Where does it exist? How does it exist?

Ontology is the science of what is. It is the science of the kinds and structures of objects, properties, events, processes and relations in every area of reality. Sometimes 'ontology' is used in a broader sense. It refers to the study of what might exist. The term 'ontology' (or ontologia) was coined in 1613, independently, by two philosophers, Rudolf Göckel (Goclenius), in his Lexicon philosophicum and Jacob Lorhard (Lorhardus), in his Theatrum philosophicum. Its first occurrence in English as recorded by the OED appears in Bailey's dictionary of 1721, which defines ontology as 'an Account of being in the Abstract.'

'Ontology seeks to provide a definitive and exhaustive classification of entities in all spheres of being. The classification should be definitive in the sense that it can serve as an answer to such questions as: What classes of entities are needed for a complete description and explanation of all the goings-on in the universe? Or: What classes of entities are needed to give an account of what makes true all truths? It should be exhaustive in the sense that all types of entities should be included in the classification, including also the types of relations by which entities are tied together to form larger wholes.

Ontological questioning has not been scrupulously raised and discussed in the study of business. This has resulted in oversimplified thinking in the attempts at expanding the horizons in the realm of knowledge. Experience was given precedence over knowledge. Craze for expansion and proliferation of business became the highest priority. Profit making and mutual competitiveness were the motivation and drive for business empire building. Ultimate business values were consumed in stress on utility. It is in this context that the following initiative has been noted.

The principle of ontology has lured the attention of experts in the sphere of Business. The Business Management Ontology (BMO) represents an integrated information model. It helps to better align IT with business. It brings together business process design, project management, requirements management, and business performance management (in the form of balanced scorecards). As such, it forms the basis for an integrated, vendor-neutral, Business Management Knowledge Base. It is from this Base various artifacts can be generated. Business analysts will be the primary users of the BMO. IT experts will also use it to establish mappings to software-related definitions, such as business objects and Web service descriptions. This is a welcome gesture.

-30-

INDIVIDUAL AND SOCIETY

An individual is a social atom. Society is an agglomeration of social atoms. We find no dependency, no bond. However, a bond emerging from the individual self interest might be undertaken. Social bonding should emerge from our interactions with each other. Language, money, and law are social entities. They rely on societies for their existence and their function.

Society is a mysterious kind of 'thing.' It's a mysterious crowd of individuals. It is less mysterious if we consider the emergence of social relations from the interactions of individuals. Such relations are the relations of communications for which we need language. We need relations of transactions whereby goods and services are traded for which we need money. We need relations of guidelines for behaviour for which we need law. Thereby we have a set of structures. Therefore, individuals are bound to each other in complex webs of relationships. These structures are fragile. They can collapse under us, though they were once in place. This makes the task of understanding and sustaining all the more important.

An economic market is one populated by homo economicus, the rational trustee of his own interests. The market would then deliver rational and efficient results. The efficient market hypothesis suggested that financial markets populated by information-sensitive, rational and competitive players, would always set prices that reflected a sum total of available knowledge. Nobody could trump the market. Government intervention would always lead to a worse outcome than if it were left to itself. Bitter experience is showing that markets are not streamlined law governed machines effortlessly pointing themselves at the best possible outcomes. The weather, or earthquakes, or turbulent flow in water pipes, chaotic, constantly at the mercy of the unpredictable and populated by players whose sentiments and beliefs are highly various and highly susceptible to infection from others.

It is this social bonding that is the main prerogative in business. Money sustains social bonding, language externalizes it, and law controls it.

-31-

STRATEGY AS LANGUAGE GAME

Strategy has the character of "language games," says Ludwig Wittgenstein. Traditional view holds: language simply "draws pictures" of an existing reality. Wittgenstein does not follow this stand. He opines that there is not any one right way to view the world. All we really have are different language games. These define the conventions by which we agree to talk or act.

Each language is at least a different "form of life." It expresses itself in different ways of speaking and acting. It does not make sense to ask whether a chosen language game is a true or false representation of reality. People find the conventions and rules of their language game as a useful way to conduct their business. Different language games prove more or less useful, depending on the situation at hand and the purpose of the players.

We call language games rhetorics. In the 1950s long-range planning was the language in vogue. In the 1960s and 1970s strategic portfolio planning and diversification became the dominant rhetoric. In the 1980s competition analysis and generic strategies came to the fore and diversification lost its charm. By the mid-1980s, the emphasis had turned to sources of competitive advantage, and restructuring. By the end of the 1980s the new slogans were strategic thinking, core competencies, global strategy, and strategic alliance. Since the beginning of 1990s, this process has become an illustrious continuum. By now, it's interesting to trace back the language games paradigm shift and discover a strategy chain as an infinite regress.

The rhetorics of strategy are introduced as new and improved ways of formulating strategy and gaining competitive advantage. A new perspective in strategy is introduced, it comes with a rhetoric: This is a new idea. This represents a radical break from the past. It warrants attention because the previous concepts are outdated and no longer relevant.

Leading edge companies have embraced it and benefited from it. If a firm wants to be leading edge, it will have a new language.

Strategy is associated with war: the tactics on which wars are won or lost. It is a militarist image. It suffuses much of the discourse on business strategy. The first book on strategy is by the Chinese military strategist, Sun-Tzu's The Art of War in the 6th Century BC. Managers are often measured in terms of the extent to which he gives the firm a corporate strategy to its competitive advantage relative to its competition.

Strategy is not something devised. It is also something that happens. It emerges constantly in a firm, as different people respond to and reinterpret their sense of the organization's identity and purpose.

-32-

RHETORIC OF SPACE AND BUSINESS

Everyday life is full of space: where we live, where we work, how we communicate. Everyday life is about the kinds of houses we live in, the kinds of houses we wish to live in, the structure of the neighbourhood and the spatial organization of the office. Do we live in gated communities? Is the store close by or do we need to drive there? Is there a public park for an early morning walk? Is the public transport system adequate?

Cultures of space are its production, consumption, and regulation. It is not a study of urban geography. It is not the phenomenology of space. It moves between spaces of residence, city development projects, and the discourses that inform, influence, and construct these spaces. It means that it is involved in the rhetoric of space employed in property development, home, and city projects of the state.

It explores how the rhetoric of space in these three kinds of spaces embodies certain cultural notions about topography, life, and economy. It is interested in the cultural construction of spaces. The rhetoric and discourses of space are mostly about projects that are in progress rather than already built areas.

Space informs life style because the geography of your home and office determines your class and social status. Where you live determines how you live. It informs your work habits and your modes of transport. A space that is not comfortable, or is surrounded by excessive noise or pollution can be emotionally and psychologically disturbing.

Space is a social construct. The social is located in space. Social space is always dynamic, constituted by social relations. Space is also about power-real or symbolic. Social space might consist of contradictory, even conflictual spaces: it is never one but many spaces.

We need discuss the spaces of property, housing, townships, and city development projects as trans-locality in the present context. Social actors like employers, employees, politicians, corporate managers, property developers interact with local and extra local institutions and social processes in the formation of relations, identities and meanings.

-33-

WELCH AND SMITH AND THEIR RHETORIC

Language is omnipresent in manager's realm. Once we try an experiment or imagine a company, a school, we need language. Language reigns supreme there. The use of language is linked to the action the manager undertakes: designing, motivating others, writing a request to the boss, sending a mail, and reading a report. However the present day manager sees all these from a different angle. He takes words for granted. He ignores words. Words to him are noises of the organization. Around us we hear differing notes on the use of language. It is the thrill of a contemporary zest and zeal for the new ways of managing; "an awe-inspiring flood of words - not all of them useful - about the coming age of enlightened organizations."

Management is rhetoric. What is it that makes certain rhetorical strategies more stirring than others? What rhetorical strategies inspire an audience to act rather than contribute to a growing sense of management hyperbole?

What is the contrast between the rhetoric of Jack Welch and Roger Smith? Welch's rhetoric has been more successful at mobilizing action rather than that of Smith.

Both of them were highly visible CEOs. They took charge of their firms in 1981. They tried to champion change, to lead their firms into the 1990s in a transformed state. Welch's rhetoric was more successful at mobilizing action. They relied heavily on promoting their visions of what such a transformation would entail. Only Welch was an expert in this game. Welch's rhetoric showed the effort typically required a deft combination of an imaginative vision of the future, a realistic portrayal of the present, and a selective depiction of the past, which can serve as a contrast to the future. There must be a "creative tension" between reality and vision that inspires people personally to take up the challenge of transformation.

In contrast, Roger Smith tried admirably to portray GM as transforming itself to become the American "21st Century Corporation." His vision of the 21st century was not spelled out in meaningful detail, therefore was uninspiring. The concept remained vague. Smith refused to face the realities of GM during the 1980s. He externalized GM's problems - there were disappointments: "dramatic shift in customer demand," "higher interest rates," and a "deteriorating economy." GM's past is portrayed as great, present as great and future as great. There was little creative tension in Smith's rhetoric.

Unlike Smith, Welch knows how to cook - and the recipe is rhetoric: metaphors and analogies, slogans and maxims. They were not merely numerical data. They were persuasive. They were combined with a powerful delivery style. Welch employed powerful metaphors and analogies to communicate his vision. He meticulously mixed analogy and metaphor to describe vividly the attempts to dismantle the old GE management system.

Organizational myths, legends, and sagas employ a different rhetorical technique. Events are drawn from an organization's history involving its employees, the function, and its past and the present. The present rhetoric is revolutionary. But it often fails. The need of the hour everywhere is, we need to find a new rhetoric which shall be for change, yes, for change to create the possibility for action.

-34-

PSYCHIC PATTERNS IN BUSINESS SPACE

"Psychic" is a word relating to the particular nature in man. This helps man perceive spatiality through senses. No sense can operate independently. It has to function with brain as a coordinating and associating factor. The brain relates touch, sight, smell, hearing and taste to thought related images. This is the key point in perception. Brain formats the visual images in the mind. It may predict the future. The mind functions as the centre of thought, emotion, and behaviour. It consciously adjusts or mediates man's responses to the social and physical environment. The word 'psychic' means relating to or being influenced by the human mind or psyche. It attempts to convey the working of the human psyche, in all its perceptional, psychological and prognosticating features. These features form patterns in minds. A pattern is a composition of traits and features characteristics of an individual or group.

Space can be segregated into the vistas of exterior space and those of interior space. Exterior space encompasses the spaces that can be grasped and perceived by the five senses, or the faculties of sight, taste, touch, hearing and smell. Interior space is perceived through the sense of the mind: metaphysical, psychological, artistic, narrative and virtual spaces. Space requires a societal and cultural background in order to be clearly conjectured. Space in this context can be broadly seen as occupying three broad areas: physical, philosophical, and experiential. These wide spectrums include manifold spatial constructs that can be identified in terms like cosmological, architectural, artistic, narrative, psychological, narrative, and business.

Man is crazy for progress. Progress depends on the growth of business too. He is yearning for newer and newer businesses: either through innovating the present or establishing the new. Understanding the present state of already existing ones will be required for that. Business can be understood ontologically if one succeeds in discovering the psychic patterns in business space. Man is always trying to innovate and improve the already existing businesses. Poor grasp of this will not let one innovate business. The innovation is taking place first in the psychic patterns in the mind. This shows that the study and evaluation of businesses are possible using the ontological existence of business: it would make the manager feel the nature and the function of business. Such a comprehension will help entrepreneurs to continuously innovate and enhance the quality of business. Innovation comprises selection and substitution. By innovation, one can select an item which demands substitution. Such an item will be substituted with the best possible from among the new ones. A continuous process of innovation would improve the quality of businesses.

-35-

JOURNAL POTENTIAL IN EDUCATION AND RESEARCH

Quite recently The Times Higher Education and Thomas Reuter released the World University Rankings. Underpinning the World University Rankings is a sophisticated exercise in information gathering and analysis. The Global University performance tables judge research-led universities across all their core missions — teaching, research, knowledge transfer, and international outlook. Thirteen carefully calibrated performance indicators provide the most comprehensive and balanced comparisons, trusted by students, academics, university leaders, industry, and governments. These thirteen performance indicators are grouped in five areas: teaching the learning environment (worth 30% of the overall ranking sore), research: volume, income, and reputation (worth 30%), citations: research influence (worth 30%), industry income: innovation (worth 2.5%), and international outlook (worth 7.5%).

Citations explain and vindicate the significance of research influence. A journal is considered the best vehicle for academic and research knowledge. Research influence (30%) is promoted by journals. It is the single most influential of the 13 indicators. It looks at the role of universities in spreading new knowledge and ideas. Scholars use this vehicle to disseminate knowledge. Research influence is examined by capturing the number of times a university's published work is cited by scholars globally. Thomas Reuter in 2013-14 examined more than fifty million citations to 6 million journal articles, published over five years. The data are drawn from the 12,000 academic journals indexed by Thomas Reuter's Web of Sciences database. They include all indexed journals published between 2007 and 2011.The citations help show how each university is contributing to the sum of human knowledge. They tell us whose research has stood out. They pronounce how research has been shared around the global scholarly community to push further the boundaries of our collective understanding, irrespective of disciplines.

All these suggest how relevant and appropriate the role of a journal in higher education and research scenario is. Researchers may avail themselves of the columns of refereed journals, prepare scientific papers, and make their contribution known to the whole world. Therefore, all well-wishers and benefactors of the academic journals shall be meticulous in the sustenance of journals in disseminating knowledge across the globe.

–36–

ENTREPRENEURSHIP AND EDUCATION

It is possible to stimulate people to think entrepreneurially. It is possible to stimulate people to engage themselves in entrepreneurial activities. Entrepreneurship is attracting the interest of Indian policy makers and the national entrepreneurial potential has become an important educational and research topic. It is interesting to note why are Indian policy makers interested in entrepreneurship? The answer is: In the present environment characterized by rapid economic change and intensified competition internally and externally, firms all over the world are under constant pressure to attain and sustain the competitive advantage. The strengthening of Indian competitiveness is our common challenge particularly as competitive pressure is coming from China and other developing countries. In this context, a well-defined strategy is inevitable. Developing entrepreneurship is a key instrument of this strategy to rejuvenate Indian innovation and competitiveness. Entrepreneurship is a driving force of economic restructuring. It moves away from the production of old products and services with low value added, obsolete technology, and obsolete organizational capabilities. It is the vehicle for the transformation of the existing enterprises and the development of new ones. It is a driving force of innovation, competitiveness, and growth. As such it also drives a nation towards the achievement of high quality of life and social prosperity.

Building up competitive advantage and maintaining sustainable high growth will depend on how much national intellectual energy and physical resources a country will be able to allocate to the creation of high quality enterprises whose competitive advantage will be based on up-to-date technological, organizational, and managerial knowledge. The challenge is the development of a consultative relationship between universities, research institutions, and industry. This means co-operation between education and training institutions on one hand, and engineers and production managers on the other, leading to an increase in the stock of entrepreneurial knowledge. Our stereotyped education system with conventional universities and affiliated technological institutions shall be transformed into new educational hubs where entrepreneurship shall be wedded to education empowering the youth to survive risks of entrepreneurship in the process.

-37-

HOLACRACY IN ACADEMIA

Holacracy is a system of organizational governance. It is a social technology. In holacracy, authority and decision-making are distributed throughout a holarchy of self-organizing teams rather than in a management hierarchy. Holacracy has been adopted in for-profit and non-profit organizations in Australia, France, Germany, New Zealand, Switzerland, the United Kingdom, and the United States.

The Holacracy system was incubated at Ternary Software, Exton, Pennsylvania, the company noted for experimenting with more democratic forms of organizational governance. In 2007 Brian Robertson distilled the best practices in management into Holacracy. In 2010 he laid out the core principles and practices of the system. In June 2015, Robertson's book, Holacracy: The New Management System for a Rapidly Changing World explained its practices. Arthur Koestler in his book The Ghost in the Machine (1967) coined holacracy from holarchy. Holarchy is composed of holons (Greek holos "whole"). Holocracy suggested "autonomous " and "self-reliant," at once dependent on the greater whole of which they form part.

Holarchy, thus, is a hierarchy of self-regulating holons that function both as autonomous wholes and as dependent parts. The building blocks of Holacracy's organizational structure are roles. Holacracy distinguishes between roles and the people who fill them, as one individual can hold multiple roles at any given time. A role is not a job description; its definition follows a clear format including a name, a purpose, and optional "domains" to control. Roles are defined by each circle—or team—via a collective governance process, getting updated regularly to adapt to the ever-evolving needs of the organization.

Holacracy specifies a structured process known as "integrative decision making" for proposing changes in governance and amending or objecting to proposals. This is not a consensus-based system, not even a consent-based system, but one that integrates relevant input from all parties and ensures that the proposed changes and objections to those changes are anchored in the roles' needs (and through them, the organization's needs), rather than people's preferences or ego. It's time for holacracy to fit in some valued space in b-school academics.

-38-

ICON, INDEX, SYMBOL

Meaning of a word is given to it using different kinds of relationships. The study of meaning is semantics. The discipline that deals with the collection and classification of meaning is semiotics. How does one arrive at meanings, what does the meaning of a text suggest, and how does one derive meanings? - All these are interesting issues.

What does the word MBA (form) generate in our mind as its meaning (content)? It appeals to our mind as "icon" of management skill and expertise. It suggests as "index" of management knowledge and experience. It relates to as "symbol" of management programme and information. It also appertains to a management degree/diploma awarded by a statutory authority.

MBA post-graduate is the icon of management: The notion of an icon is a case of replacement. The form of the word replaces the person with management attributes: dexterity and astute expediency in the execution of skills which one has acquired in a b-school. It is the inherent property of the form that gets externalized in the person. In flesh, blood, and bone, he must be a prospective, potential manager. He becomes an icon: the management expertise incarnate. Such a product rolls out of b-schools of the stature of an IIM, IIFT, ISB, XLRI, SYMBIOSIS, SCMS-COCHIN, and other like institutions.

MBA postgraduate is an index of management: Notion of the index is a case of sequence. The merit of the person is unraveled through the connected sequence one leading to the other. One manifestation of knowledge is let known to others through experiential events. One after the other every activity will expose his managerial ingenuity and competence. He will show how managerial situations are handled with vivacity and propriety. As we witness smoke we infer that there is fire so we see the managerial performance, we confirm the competence behind. There are many b-schools of the second order, which produce MBAs to the level of index.

MBA is a symbol of management: A symbol of management presumes that it is a partial replacement. The information and programme in a b-school may have influenced him, but to the core the transformation may not have affected. Partially the training has had its influence. The symbol also performs well at times when occasion demands. This solely depends on the individual, not solely owing to the b-school. Many of the b-schools train students to this level.

The fourth one called "others" forms the category of MBA which gives the person an appellation MBA. That's all. The qualities of the three levels of icon, index, and symbol may be found lacking in this. Hundreds of b-schools and the b-departments of some universities and colleges produce such meanings to the MBA.

As "each tree is known by its fruit," so is the b-school known by its products.

-39-

COMPUTER LITERATE AND INFORMATION LITERATE

Scientific modes of knowledge have undergone great changes. Information technology has also developed along similar lines. In other words, the Internet has been using its supportive role for these changes in our research and social life. To be precise, the Internet has been a powerful medium in research activities and has been transforming society. Yes, consequent on these, we have been experiencing both internationalization and globalization. There has been a growing demand for inter-trans disciplinary strategies and methods for that. Therefore scholars in humanities and social sciences have had to work together to meet the growing demands.

Digital resources are extensively distributed across a range of sites: libraries, museums, traditional and digital archives, websites etc. They are catalogued according to very different practices and standards that reflect in some combination: the resources' initial location, their intellectual content, and their physical form. Presently, internet accessible resources are located by users who know how and where to find them.

All of us must acknowledge and address the problem and form a community of interests to formulate the needs and desires. If we ignore the changes going on and the requirements that they cause, we risk being left out. We risk being provided with information, organized according to the needs or conceptions of information engineers or natural scientists.

Within this entire struggle for information on the World Wide Web, another tool of the Internet, e-mail has been widely used, also within the humanities, making contacts between scholars and students faster and easier, no matter which geographical distance may separate them.

Mailing list, Twitter, Facebook, WhatsApp ,etc. as forums of (permanent) discussion form new communities united solely by their fields of interest. Everybody may enter-without respect of person or position - as soon as he or she knows where the discussion is held and how to subscribe - as soon as he or she has access to the Internet. But generally taking part in the discussion is once a question of computer literacy as the ability to find lists where topics you are interested in are treated. Furthermore, participants are pointed towards new publications, online and printed, appearing in the field, and receive comments on new features of the Internet and new software for different purposes.

During the past many decades we became computer literate. Now during the last few decades we have felt the need to become information literate and we have been vying with one another to achieve the goal. It all shows Computer Literate and Information Literate is complementary to each other. Shall we have introspection: despite all information surpluses how far we have trapped information with propriety?

-40-

SETTING DIRECTION, CREATING ALIGNMENT, AND GAINING COMMITMENT

Effective leadership, to John Ryan formerly the Chancellor of the State University of New York, involves three key components: setting direction, creating alignment, and gaining commitment. It's important that leaders set a direction and they encourage people to follow in that direction. The best people do it well and others not so well. What people most want in a leader is someone who is authentic, who they trust. People now are educated and intelligent and well-read and they see through people who are/or may be as genuine as they should be. Authentic leaders start with the courage of their convictions — they are not holding polls or taking surveys. They obviously listen to people's news and integrate them but they also have to get the vision and the direction. They have to understand what direction this particular organization needs to go in.

Creative leadership involves people thinking beyond the boundaries that limit individuals and organizations and if you think about that it extends beyond the typical skills that are associated with routine leadership. Business schools teach people how to analyze data, coach employees, even projects. We try to go beyond that and teach people how to be innovative. And we do that through three elements: assessment, challenge and support.

Advancing Global Leadership is the thinking and emphasis behind this new initiative. People who are involved in global leadership positions are today facing greater complaints in their roles, whether it is at the mid-level or higher level in their organizations. They need to perceive new situations they face, culturally as well as organizationally, with the people they interact with and they have to adapt their leadership style accordingly.

Leadership potential is a "muscle" that needs exercise to develop. What is the best sort of exercise? First of all, one has to commit to it. One can't be a leader if he/she is not going to work at it, practice it. You don't become good football players unless you practise and you don't become a good leader unless you practise. The best way to become a leader is a yearning to become one, to read about it, look for a mentor or a coach, go to a programme and practise those skills. Behaviours are very important in becoming a leader.

Eleanor Roosevelt was born into a wealthy family but was orphaned when she was ten and had a terrible childhood. She became the person who started the Civil Rights Movement and the Women's Right Movement. She had tremendous compassion for the poor. She helped the entire world. She was chair of the UN Committee that drafted the Universal Declaration of Human Rights. Most important she did not take public opinion polls to see what she thought was right.

Mahatma Gandhi practised what he preached at every possible level. He treated others with great concern. In his letters and writings to others to the world and even to young children, never had a patronizing or "holier than thou" element, and always looked at everyone as equals. More importantly though was his ability to articulate a vision in a language that they understood and were inspired by.

-41-

NEW DAWN FOR DEVELOPMENT

During the early years of this millennium, in the European Union there was an awakening: they decided to halt the loss of biodiversity. At once, they resolved to reverse the loss of biodiversity. These resolutions have transformed Europe into the most entrepreneurial region in the world, into the most innovative realm. The Gothenburg Declaration and the Lisbon Agenda showed yearning for attainment of these aspirations leading to business growth and environmental diversity. Initially, they had appeared to be probable ground for conflict. But they turned out to be fertile source: a whole new range of business opportunities cropped up: new grass roots models of corporate good citizenship.

Probioprise brought together business and environment. It led to the establishment of European Small and Medium-sized enterprises. As we all know probioprise is an acronym: it stands for pro-biodiversity enterprise. A probiodversity SME is one which is dependent on biodiversity for its core business and it contributes to biodiversity conservation through that core business. Many firms involved in probioprise try to combine profit-making, delivering social benefits, and enhancing biodiversity.

In India, business growth and environmental sensitivity are perceived to be unlikely bedfellows. India's politicians, it seems, have not heard this aphorism; politics is the art of the possible. Our ministers have their special priorities: their caste, their community, their class, or their creed. Prejudices for their own convictions will of course lead them to prejudices against those of others. Very often they seem to be in potential conflict with each other. However, in the horizon, new rays of hope start rising in the wake of a new elected government with absolute majority, astute confidence and remarkable resolution. Let's leave the wrong priorities and load our youth's minds with innovative ideas!

Our b-schools can initiate further discussions in this area - probioprise - to find out beneficial spill over effects for other kinds of environmentally oriented firms, for social enterprise, and for understanding and for support for SMEs generally.

–42–

LET THE BUYER BEWARE!

What are my rights? It is a point of information, meaning, what I may do according to the rules of some association or some body politic, and where the rules that are written down and understood are. I may have the right to bring one guest in, but not two. I have the right to use the pavement, but not to obstruct it. Different rights may be accorded to different people. A citizen can vote in an election, but not a foreigner. Rights, here, are a matter of what rules permit.

Societies evolve systems of permission on the one hand, and boundaries that must not be crossed on the other. We can understand the evolution of systems of promise-giving and keeping, systems of property, and eventually systems of law. We realize that we have different "positive" rights. It means: systems of boundaries and permissions, and the systems of status that mean that others must forbear from behaving in various ways. All of these are social constructions, in the sense that they owe their existence to the actions and habits of the society.

The adjective "right" as in "the right thing to do" or as in "the right decision," is fine. As right becomes a noun and people start to talk about rights, everything goes pear-shaped. The moral is that we have to be careful. Ordinary talk of rights as established and enshrined in custom and law, is fine. Advocating particular policies and changes is fine. Using the language of rights is a perfectly reasonable way of attempting to persuade each other of the merits of a policy. But thinking of rights, however cloudily, as affording some kind of metaphysical basis for our advocacy, is not. Thinking of a calculus of rights, unique and visible to people of reason everywhere, is dangerous in many directions. The more confident one is of a kind of moral calculus of detailed rights will lead to the spectre of imperialism. The language of rights occupies something of the role of a new proselytizing religion, impatient of the existence of infidels, anxious to globalize its own discoveries and to suppress whatever variations and alternatives have evolved elsewhere. The problem lies with people's hearts, their fears, envies, prejudices and historical enmities, rather than their heads.

When you buy something, you must have precautions against being cheated. You cannot trust merchants to be honest about what they sell. Let the buyer beware when shopping for a used car. Several among the lamps among those a dealer offered were broken. "If a customer isn't smart enough to try a lamp before he buys it, that's his problem." The dealer argued:"Let the buyer beware!"

-43-

SUPER TRENDS IN BUSINESS

Success in the business world tomorrow means recognizing the sweeping changes of today. Many new trends occur in the global market place comprising Karl Albrecht's "Super Trends."

Customer Super trend focuses on the Micro-segmentation in the Marketplace: Monolithic markets, customer segments, and product categories are continually breaking up into smaller clusters of demand and preference. Customers are becoming ever more differentiated in their lifestyles, and interests, with smaller and more specialized groups. They respond to more narrowly targeted commercial messages. An example of this micro-segmentation can be seen in the rapid rise of blogs or online personal diaries and new columns.

Competitor Super trend deals with value targeting: It aims for whatever matters most to individual consumers. Enterprises which offered a broad range of products or services are now facing specialized competitors providing more specific, targeted solutions, often in two ways and at lower prices. Economic Super trend is built on Chinafication. China's vast pool of cheap labour may dominate world labour markets for decades, giving a near permanent monopoly on cheaply manufactured goods.

Technological Super trend suggests a shift from Information to Knowledge. Today, information is a profitless commodity and knowledge is the new competitive advantage. A shift from industrial based societies to information based societies is noted.

Knowledge workers are renamed as data workers. No value is added to the processing of information. The developing state of all-pervasive connectedness imposed by internet use may give rise to a greater appetite for meaningful human contact.

Special Super trend is of Dumb and Dirty. Media environment is forcing marketers of the popular culture to resort to more provocative methods of capturing the attention of the jaded public. It creates a pervasive culture amusement that tends to develop and displace thoughtful discourse. The evermore desperate use of sexualized and violent content as an attention getting strategy in news, advertising, publishing, and entertaining is causing more people to perceive the social values projected by the popular commercial culture as narcissist, hedonistic, anti-intellectual and regressive.

Special Super trend: "Cyber mobbing" speaks about web communities emerging as "smart mobbing" and swarm advocacy spawning temporary or transient political entities that outflank traditional channels and methods of influence. Political segment is becoming much more popular in the broadest media. Specialized advocacy groups form and disintegrate over time. Elected officials and public agencies fall under scrutiny. Political activists can assemble temporary constituencies through online marketing and fund raising. Web based news producers are outpacing traditional radio; TV broadcast sources, and the print media.

Legal Super trend generates Knowledge Warfare. Competitive struggles are fought between knowledge intensive enterprises. They are fought on the legal battlefield and in the market place. The creators, producers, publishers, distributors, and consumers of intellectual property based products pursue their separate interests. High profile law suits have highlighted the increasing vulnerability of copyrights and other intellectual property protections.

Geophysical Super trend points to Counter Americanism. Threats of violence against Americans and US enterprises are significantly increasing the cost of business operations. As the US continues to lose its unique competitive advantages in science and technology, as intellectual capital continues to develop rapidly in competing countries, such as China and India, and as competition for oil and other natural resources intensifies, an American "twilight" of influence is almost likely.

–44–

WE BRISTLE WHEN WE ARE BRIDLED

We have reached a stage when we are disturbed by too much management, at once too little freedom. More executives assume that they are managers.

They are paid, to oversee, control, and administer. The tools of management can compel people to be obedient and diligent. They can't make people creative and committed. In recent years there is a lot of rhetoric about involvement, empowerment, and self-direction. In many companies, employees are referred to as "associates" or "team members." But ask yourselves: Do they have more freedom to design their jobs? Do they have more discretion to choose the work of their choice? We bristle when we are bridled.

We are worried about too much hierarchy, at the same time too little community. We are energized by work when the work involved a group of people bound by their devotion to common cause, undeterred by lack of resources and undaunted by expertise. Hierarchies are good at aggregating effort. Hierarchies are not good at mobilizing effort. When it comes to mobilizing human capability, communities outperform bureaucracies. In bureaucracy the basis for exchange is contractual (pay for work). In community, you are a partner in cause. In bureaucracy, you are a factor of production. In bureaucracy, loyalty is a product of economic dependence.

We are shocked to see too much exhortation, at once too little purpose: Initiative, creativity, and passion are gifts. They are benefactions employees choose, day by day and moment by moment, to give or withhold. They cannot be commanded. By exhorting people to work more, or harder, by loving their customers and killing their competitors, you will not get their initiative, creativity, and passion for the company. You'll elicit these capabilities through your approach. You ask yourselves: What kind of purpose the best of everyone who works here? What lofty cause would inspire folks to give generously of their talents?

−45−
CREATIVITY

Thinking involves a set of mental skills. These skills in a person create, manipulate, and communicate to others the personal symbols of mental life. Thinking is a set of processes whereby people assemble, use and revise mental symbolic models. One can model the layout of a city in the mind's eye in order to plan a route to navigate from one location to another. Or one can model the workings of a car to begin to determine what is causing the frighteningly loud noise under the bonnet. Thinking occurs internally or mentally, but is generally inferred indirectly through behaviour. The thinking involved in writing, can be inferred by asking the writer to think aloud and analyzing the text produced. Thinking is a process that entails manipulating representations of what we know about the world.

What we think or know about a topic is often directed at the solution of specific tangible goals. A writer's thoughts must be goal directed, if a text is ever to emerge. Directed thinking specifies a goal to be achieved in the near future, directed thought works towards it. The example is an on-the-job task, an order from the boss to complete a routine memorandum in sales projections.

Undirected thought meanders, without progress toward a clearly identified goal. Dreaming, daydreaming, and artistic thinking are examples. Recurrent thinking is characterized by repetitious thoughts that may occur while awake or asleep.

Creative thinking and critical thinking share many similar components. But they take on each a different organization and purpose. Traditionally, a creative act is one that is original, useful in some sense, and dependent on special training, education, and abilities. Creative thinking focuses more on the product. Process and product creativity are two different concepts. Process creativity refers to the ability to apply relevant knowledge inventively to problem at hand. It is normal like remembering. Product creativity refers to the quality and quantity of works judged by others as original, innovative, useful, and important. People are creative in the process sense; few are creative in the product sense. Anyone can create symbols, but the genius creates symbols that others pay attention to time and again. Product creativity depends not only on individual ability but also on the cultural and societal support available to the individual. It occurs only when the right individual lands in the right discipline at the right place and at the right time. A b-school student acquires skills of thinking and will be a master in both process creativity and product creativity.

–46–

EMPOWER NURSES FOR HEALTH CARE MANAGEMENT

Nursing is the largest segment of healthcare workforce. It has been evolving from 'home visiting and community-based care' to 'hospital and institution-based care.' Nurses spend the greatest amount of time in delivering patient care as a profession. They therefore have valuable insights and unique abilities to contribute as partners with other health care professionals in improving the quality and safety of care. The Future of Nursing explores how nurses' roles, responsibilities, and education should change significantly to meet the increased demand for care that will be created by healthcare reform and to advance improvements in World's increasingly complex health system.

Nurses should be fully engaged with other health professionals and assume leadership roles in redesigning care in the world. Nurses have embraced the latest healthcare changes. A long-time hurdle facing the predominantly female profession is nursing's lacking power compared to that of the physicians and hospital administrators. As women make continuous inroads across the board, this more traditional issue will fade away.

Public opinion polls always favour nurses. Nurses are among the best trusted professions. Nurses will remain in a favourable position with the public if they chip away at the fragmentation of care that exists in the healthcare profession. Nurses are in an ideal position to accomplish this, given their holistic view of health care.

Today large challenges and opportunities face this profession. Besides upholding high standards of patient care, there is the need to increase the visibility, respect, and recognition of nursing while maintaining its important role in health care delivery and research. Nursing is an invisible profession to the public. Nurses often feel reluctant to communicate their worth to the public for social reasons, and may discount the important contributions they make. They are reduced to "physician extenders," "handmaidens," or "physician substitutes." Medicine is concerned with diagnosing and treating illnesses; nursing is concerned with both of these, as well as the patient's response to both health and illness, including the environment and family. Nurses cannot substitute for physicians or physicians for nurses. They provide complementary care. Among the various functionaries of the healthcare system, the nurse is the nerve centre. The soothing presence of the nurse forms the main stream of healthcare. It is the nurse who imparts to the patient continuous care and caress. The ephemeral presence of a physician, surgeon, pharmacist, laboratory technician and the sustained presence of a nurse with the patient will sooner or later make the nurse the king/queen pin of the medical care system. This necessitates need for a managerial stream to supervise and oversee the medical care system. A panacea for all these is: start courses in nursing management in b-schools and provide intensive training to those chosen nurses befitting to become prospective managers of medical care management. It will reinforce the skills and trainings and to strengthen the confidence and visibility of nurses to take over managing hospital and nursing care meticulously.

-47-

INVOKE SOLAR ENERGY: SAVE THE UNIVERSE!

Energy is life giver. It is life sustainer. It is life destroyer. The Sun is life-giver, life sustainer, and life destroyer all together. The prime source of energy in the cosmos is the Sun. All living and non-living things on earth owe their being to the Sun. The Sun, therefore, is the physical presence of the cause of life on earth.

Have we properly 'understood' the significance of this prime energy provider?

In the olden days, there were ancient cultures which had deemed the Sun the supreme power. Some cultural reminiscences and practices from the Vedic days could substantiate Indians' acceptance of such valued knowledge: people used to worship the prime source of energy and offered prayers. The Vedic Hymn Ohm Bhur Bhuvah Swvaha is an invocation to the omniscient, the omnipresent, and the omnipotent and, and obviously it's sung in praise of the Sun.

But, human manipulation of political power has been manoeuvring knowledge in a way that didn't let the world tap solar resources cleverly.

People started tapping energy from water, from coal, from oil, from nuclear active materials, and from wind. Direct energy source, solar energy, was ignored at all levels. The world powers that promoted marketing energy grew economically powerful. All these are not perennially reliable sources.

It is in this context that a novel re-conceptualization of knowledge related to energy becomes mandatory and the prudent use of this knowledge demands our attention. We will acknowledge: the Sun is the power that protects and sustains us; the Sun is our god as the Sun is the supreme power; and the Sun is the infinite source of energy.

The B-schools will take up the responsibility to study more and research more and more on solar energy resources, and tap the resources for power generation. The B-school syllabus and curriculum will have to be in tune with solar power generation and distribution. We can use this abundance in energy for the development of our planet: in the production of food materials and other essential requirements.

-48-

RIVER OF TIME

'What is time? If nobody asks me, I know; but if I desired to explain it to any one who should ask me, then plainly I know not,' says St. Augustine.

We are creatures of time. We live our lives in time. Our attempts to grasp time itself seem to run into an impasse.

We think of time following by: We talk of the river of time. We talk of time passing by. We talk of time yet to come. The image is of the moving present.

One moment in this year is present as I write this. But it has no sooner come than it is gone. The special moment, the present, is moving inexorably onwards.

Time flows. What rate does it flow at? Time seems to have no option but to go as it does: one second per second.

The rate at which time flows is suspect. And also the direction it flows in. We imagine the present creeping up on events which are still in the future. Is time flowing not forwards but backwards?

The past has gone; the future is yet to be, so there is only the present.

We think of the present as singled out from all the others. It's the one that is special. It looks that it is the only one that really exists.

Philosophers generally incline to the view that it is best to avoid the metaphor of time's flow and the special nature of the present altogether. All events, past, present, and future exist like flies in amber, with greater or lesser distances between them.

If time's flow is unreal, then what is to prevent us thinking that current events may cause previous ones? Why not we think the later omlette caused the earlier eggs to be broken?

Despite what the philosophers say, one thing is sure in the modern world: the present is the one which is real. It goads us on. It sustains us. It gives us charge. It is the magical force that gives us drive in the sphere of business.

−49−

MANAGEMENT, MANAGER, AND MANAGE

Management, manager, and manage first appear in English in the late sixteenth century. It's in the time of Shakespeare. They derive ultimately from a Latin word **manus** literally *hand* with its connotations "power" and "jurisdiction." In the late middle Ages we find the Italian word *maneggiare* begins to appear in the sixteenth century as well. In English, the term management for a long time referred in general terms to the controlling and direction of affairs. From the seventeenth century on there were literally hundreds of books published with management in their titles, referring to everything from agriculture to forestry, to healthcare, to children's education, and to prisons. By the middle of the seventeenth century, the word was being applied to business and financial matters as well. Management in its original meaning meant 'to do' and more importantly 'to cause to be done.' Today management associates itself with guiding, leading, planning, controlling, directing, and coordinating, and so on.

Now we tend to think of management as being a separate discipline. This was not always true. A century ago, as fully fledged theories of management were constructed after Victorian scientific revolution, managers or management academics borrowed profusely from engineering, natural science, military science, politics, law, economics, sociology, psychology, and even literature and the fine arts.

Harrington Emerson, the first management guru claimed that his ideas on management had been drawn from the study three thoughts: the conducting of symphony orchestras, the breeding of racehorses, and railway time tables.

Many people love to think that management has no past, whereas scientists, lawyers, philosophers, artists, political leaders, and many other professionals see themselves as part of a long tradition. Managers perversely refuse to acknowledge their heritage. In so doing, they miss out on their discipline's origin. We forget the rich diversity of influences that has made management what it is today. Whether we like it or not , we owe at least part of our present knowledge to past pioneers.

Why these thoughts, not too odd, flash in our mind today as we think of management education? We are not sure of a m-pedagogy replete with with resources drawn from the past, rich in traditional knowledge. History of management shall be the base for the strong structure of modern management erudition.

-50-

A GOOD MANAGER: A GOOD AND WELL EDUCATED PERSON

"A good manager is nothing more or less than a good and well educated person," so says Mathew Stewart in his Management Myth. He gives an insightful romp through the entire history of thinking about management.

There are two kinds of books on management: the kind that the business school professors inflict on their students and the other kind that people actually buy, the works of so-called management gurus.

The conventional view holds that management is a kind of technology, a bundle of techniques, based on scientific observation, tended by experts, and transferred to students.

Beginning in the early 1980s, a reverberating sound could be heard in elite university campuses. It was coming from the "world's newest profession."

Management consulting dates from the early decades of the twentieth century. In 1800, the consulting industry employed 18,000 professionals worldwide. In 1825, it employed about 1, 80,000 professionals worldwide. Today, it employs number unlimited like stars.

To Mathew Stewart, life is full of surprises. That's mostly a good thing. Every surprise is an opportunity for learning. A management consultant has a career replete with a long list of opportunities. Every consultant owes his/her education to the extraordinary generosity of clients.

How can so many who know so little make so much by telling other people how to do the jobs they are paid to know how to do? Stewart opines.

What makes for a good manager? A good manager is someone with a facility for analysis and an even greater talent for synthesis. He is one who has an eye both for the details and for the one big thing that really matters after internalizing the details. He is one who is able to reflect on facts in a disinterested way. He is always dissatisfied with pat answers and the conventional wisdom. He is therefore one who takes a pleasure in knowledge itself. He is someone with a wide knowledge of the way people work. He is someone who knows how to treat people with respect, honesty, integrity, trustworthiness. He is someone who knows the things which make up character. He is someone in short who understands oneself and the world around. He is someone who knows how to make the world better. All these suggest management myth is not merely a myth but a must for managers to scan, chew, and digest and then render into real life.

-51-

B SCHOOL AND CULTURAL STUDIES

B academic course and curriculum may be incomplete if there is no academic acquaintance with current conceptions of culture, yes, of popular culture. It's the culture of the masses; the culture of everyday life of the large number of people (graffiti, comic books, mass cinema, popular music, and the open spaces of the city).The mass culture was used pejoratively in the past. The culture of the "elite," then was the "true culture." For b students, it is desirable to focus on the discourses of present day shopping, the organization of shopping experience, and the ideologies of consumption. Study of shopping can be learnt only in specific contexts of economy and spending.

The cultural studies argue that culture is about the meanings a society generates. Cultural Studies believes the culture of a community includes various aspects economic, spatial, ideological, erotic, and political. Culture is not a natural thing, it is something produced. Cultural Studies is interested in production and consumption of culture. The production and consumption of culture relates to matters of class (who decides on what produced), matters of economy (who can afford it) matters of representation (how is the artifact marketed/presented). The production and consumption of cultural artifacts defines one's identity. It depends on the ability to do so and the ways in which artifacts have been marketed and sold. In short, culture is a product: made, marketed, and consumed. The analysis of society and the condition of production spilled over into the analysis of culture. Culture, now, is the mode of generating meanings and ideas. The mode is the negotiation over which the meanings are valid. Meanings are governed by power relations. We do not buy product/object. Instead, we buy a lifestyle. It locates us in a class. This is a model of selling. Let us examine contemporary advertisements for consumer objects. They suggest that acquisition of an object marks certain lifestyle: nuclear family, the working woman. It is called the ideology of consumerism.

All these vindicate a conscious awareness of the tenets of cultural studies is imperative among b students.

-52-

HARMONY IN TRIUNE: ART, SCIENCE, AND CRAFT

Management is a practice. It combines art, science, and craft. Art encourages creativity. It leads to "insights" and "vision." Science provides order. It is achieved through systematic analyses and assessment. Craft makes connections. It is reached through building tangible experiences. Art tends to be inductive. It flows from specific events to broad overviews. Science is deductive. It deduces from general concepts to specific applications. Craft is iterative. It moves back and forth between the specific and the general.

Each approaches strategy as a process of visioning in art, planning in science, and venturing in craft. Effective managing requires all these.

Propriety demands their presence in perfect balance. They have to reinforce each other. They should complement each other. Art and craft sans systematic scrutiny of science can lead to disorganized managing. Craft and science sans creative vision of art may lead to dispirited managing, careful and connected, but lacking spirit. Craft and science sans the creative vision of art can lead to dispirited managers, careful and connected, but lacking spark.

Art with science, creative and systematic without the experience of craft can produce rootless, impersonal disconnected managers. Effective managing tends to happen when the three exist, yes, co-exist.

There is carping critique on MBA education of today. It is sans craft. It prefers analytics to experience. It is weak in art. Many MBA graduates carry this imbalance to their careers. They choose jobs that favor analytics. Thus they are removed from the experience of craft. They carry this to positions in the executive suite.

It's interesting to note that a primary unit of management is a triangular format, a triune that subsumes art, science, and craft. Every unit of management shall comprise these triune basic components. The idea discussed is the reworking on one of the gems of ideas manifested in Henry Mintzberg's Managers Not MBAs, a hard look at the soft practice of managers and management development.

-53-

LADY JUSTICE UNDER CYBER THREAT

The Lady Justice carries the scale, a sword or scroll and she is often blindfolded. The blindfolded "Lady Justice" holding the beam balance, is familiar to everyone's mind. She symbolizes this profession so universally that it is important for every lawyer, judge and even support system entering the profession to understand its significance.

The Lady Justice is a metaphorical personification of the moral force in judicial systems. Her attributes are a blindfold, a balance, and a sword. The Scales of Justice represents the balance of the individual against the needs of society and a fair balance between interests of one individual and those of another. The Sword represents the enforcement measures of Lady Justice.

The blindfold today, probably her most famous symbol, first appeared in the fifteenth century. The blindfold represents decisions of objectivity and/or impartial decision or decision not influenced by wealth, politics, popularity or infamy. Blind Justice is the theory that law should be viewed objectively with the determination of innocence or guilt made without bias or prejudice. Martin Luther King Junior said, "Injustice anywhere is a threat to justice everywhere." Justice shall be meted out to every one without fear or favour. For that, judges require evidences. In the light of technological progress, nature and function of evidences undergo changes.

The incorporation of technology into the justice system is the need of the hour. Offering court services electronically or through the use of electronics within the court rooms or the disputation resolution purposes are also welcome gestures. This is due to cyber sciences.

Cyber technology is a great boon to managing business. At the same time manipulation of cyber knowledge can be bane to managing business. In response to calls from cyber professionals, the state-of the-art practices in intelligence, forensics, and cyber operations, Cybernetics offers advanced knowledge and hands-on experience in intelligence, critical infrastructure, and investigative principles as they relate to cyber intelligence. Cyber security teaches to proactively address ever-changing attack and infiltration techniques. Training in critical thinking and skills in decision-making shall be reinforced with application of cyber technology to field operations ethics as applied to cyber security operations as policy.

A practical knowledge of cybercrime investigations including methods of maintaining the integrity of cyber evidence is the cultural imperative in business education in the wake of growing cybercrimes. Therefore business education may consider cyber technologies: as modules in modern justice studies. Therefore, business education shall consider including cyber technology, cyber security, cybercrime, and cyber justice as mandatory fields of learning.

-54-

"MUNDANE" AND "INSPIRING"

The boss speaks on management. The boss may be Jack Welch or Steve Balmer or anyone else. Tom Peters edits and publishes all that is spoken by them in a book Boss Talk, where bosses tell, to our surprise, only earth earthy things.

"Mundane" (common sense) and "Inspiring" (uncommon sense) are the words that brighten the world of bosses' words.

Jack Welch of General Electric did better than everyone else during the last century. Despite that, he tells of his secret as no secret. Though the size of GE is astonishing, his executives think of themselves as running a grocery store. They will instinctively make the correct decisions if they focus on the basics of people and customers, and service and innovation. Is it that simple? What Jack means is simple: One has to focus on or shall have an obsession with the basics, within the context of the particular enterprise. For him a company is a place of ideas. It is not a place of positions. As any business matures, it runs into problems of hierarchy. Jack Welch speaks on motivation: "tell people to never allow themselves to become victims They should go somewhere else if that's how they feel." "Promote your best performers and weed out your worst. "Challenge them to give every growth idea they've got." "You can't just reward with trophies. Reward them in the wallet, too."

Steve Ballmer was Microsoft MD. He was also a spokesman of simplicity. Clear thought and leading proposition are the terms he uses. A few things he has to focus on: You make sure that that you have great people. You have to rededicate yourselves to these great people. You have to refocus on clear, simple goals. The principles we talk about will not change, the value we uphold will never change. Goals are things that change.

Rebecca Buckman in The Wall Street Journal comments: Steve Ballmer's dictum is "Simplify Goals, Heed Key Employees' Concerns."

-55-

MYTH AND MANAGEMENT

Memory is the mother of Muses. Mythology draws on our old memories. Mythology has always fascinated the mind of the common man. Mythology has lured the attention of the artist, the writer, and the thinker.

Myth is a story that originated in ancient times. It is about early history of people or, explaining natural events in the past. Muses are nine goddesses of arts, literature, and creativity

Myth touches on man's basic relation to the world and to his fellowmen. Myth touches on his original roots. Myth touches on his future possibilities and destiny.

Myth has cast a spell on the very ages which denied it. Like the severed head of Orpheus, it goes on singing even in death. The myth has perennial appeal. It has vitality of mythical thinking. It makes us feel that in all civilizations men feel several situations, similar experiences. Myth therefore makes for One World. Myth applies "a symbolic memory and symbolic hope, and an allegorical account of the perils of the way."

Myth unfolds the living chain. The chain connects the recurrent recognition scenes of the human drama.

They assure that we are not strangers in this world. We are not alone in the world.

George Santayana says:"a country without a memory is a country of mad men. Those who cannot learn from history are doomed to repeat it."

A study of myths provides, to a great extent, the origins of ideas and approaches. It traces the development of ideas. It provides a conceptual framework that will enhance the process of integration. It contributes to a more logical coherent picture of the present. It should therefore equip the perceptive person with additional alternative answers to build into his decision making model. It facilitates intellectual flexibility and a mental set for the intellectual flexibility of change through the study of myths.

Present management pedagogy can be improved. Knowledge can be expanded. Insights are gained by examining the lives and labours of management's intellectual forefathers. Theory is a legitimate goal in any discipline. It is based on the warp and woof of men's ideas in the fabric of management as given by myths.

www.ingramcontent.com/pod-product-compliance
Lightning Source LLC
Chambersburg PA
CBHW021547200526
45163CB00016B/2748